Nicky Epstein
❁Knits for Dolls

Nicky Epstein
❋Knits for Dolls
25 Fun, Fabulous Outfits for 18-Inch Dolls

 Nicky & Epstein Books   AN IMPRINT OF SIXTH&SPRING BOOKS NEW YORK

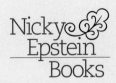

AN IMPRINT OF SIXTH&SPRING BOOKS
161 AVENUE OF THE AMERICAS, NEW YORK NY 10013
SIXTHANDSPRINGBOOKS.COM

EDITORIAL DIRECTOR
JOY AQUILINO

DEVELOPMENTAL
EDITOR
LISA SILVERMAN

ART DIRECTOR
DIANE LAMPHRON

EDITORIAL
ASSISTANT/STYLIST
JOHANNA LEVY

YARN EDITOR
CHRISTINA BEHNKE

INSTRUCTIONS
EDITORS
AMY POLCYN
SANDI PROSSER
NANCY HENDERSON
LORI STEINBERG

TECHNICAL
ILLUSTRATIONS
LORETTA DACHMAN

DESIGN/ART
PRODUCTION
DEBORAH GRISORIO

STILL PHOTOGRAPHY
JACK DEUTSCH

PROP STYLIST
DIANE LAMPHRON

VICE PRESIDENT
TRISHA MALCOLM

PUBLISHER
CARRIE KILMER

PRODUCTION
MANAGER
DAVID JOINNIDES

PRESIDENT
ART JOINNIDES

CHAIRMAN
JAY STEIN

Cataloging-in-Publication data
is available from the Library of Congress.

ISBN 978-1-936096-54-1

MANUFACTURED IN CHINA

1 3 5 7 9 10 8 6 4 2

First Edition

Contents

Ruffles and Roses
page 14

A Walk in the Woods
page 20

Petite Parisienne
page 24

Perfect Match
page 27

A Rose Is a Rose
page 30

All That Glitters
page 35

Fairy-Tale Blanket
page 40

Mirror, Mirror
page 44

Skullduggery
page 51

Modern Masterpiece
page 54

What a Hoot!
page 58

Lounging in Luxury
page 61

School Days
page 64

My Cozy Valentine
page 70

All Dolled Up
page 74

Vintage Bunny
page 77

Picnic in the Park
page 78

Grab Bag

Mix and match these adorable purse designs
with your favorite outfits.

RUFFLES AND ROSES
page 19

COAT OF MANY COLORS
page 94

TINY DANCER
page 98

MIRROR, MIRROR
page 50

PICNIC IN THE PARK
page 80

MODERN MASTERPIECE
page 56

A ROSE IS A ROSE
page 34

STRIPES AHOY
page 103

Introduction

Little girls love to play with dolls! I certainly did,
and now I love to design for them.

The 18-inch dolls featured in this book have soared in popularity in recent
years, and they're the perfect size to show off knitted fashions.

In this book you'll find a closetful. The outfits I've created range from casual
to formal, tomboy to princess, and they're all fun to knit and fun to
accessorize. In fact, many of the projects include dainty knitted
accessories, from purses to hats to socks.

I've created these designs as I create designs for children:
to be unique, fashionable, and fun to wear. After all,
the dolls of our children are like their children, and dressing the dolls in
these fashions will give them a whole new personality and a closer
connection with their "play mommies."

These knits for dolls are a wonderful opportunity for adults and
children to learn, have fun, and be creative together. You can inspire
a child to discover the joy of knitting as you work and then play
together in a fashionable world that you create.

Everyone likes to play dress-up . . . even us big girls. Happy knitting!

NICKY EPSTEIN

The
Knits for Dolls
Collection

Ruffles and Roses

A knitted basket of pink roses is the perfect accessory for this sweet-as-candy ensemble.

MATERIALS

- 1 1¾oz/50g skein (each approx 109yd/100m) of Sassy Skein *Key West Karibbean Kotton* DK weight (cotton) each in #106 flamingo (A), #130 bubblegum (B), and #125 pink coral (C)
- Small amount green yarn
- One pair size 3 (3.25mm) needles, OR SIZE REQUIRED FOR GAUGE
- Size C-2 (2.75mm) crochet hook
- 5 small snaps
- Stitch markers

GAUGE

22 sts and 32 rows to 4"/10cm over St st using size 3 (3.25mm) needles. *Take time to check gauge.*

K1, P1 RIB

(over an even number of sts)
ROW 1 (RS) *K1, p1; rep from * to end.
Rep row 1 for k1, p1 rib.

3-NEEDLE JOIN

With RS of layers facing and the needles parallel, insert a third needle into the first st on each needle and knit the two sts together.

NOTES

1) Body of top is made in one piece to armhole.
2) Skirt is made in one piece with center back seam.

SKIRT
FIRST RUFFLE

With A, cast on 108 sts. Knit 1 (WS) row. Starting with a knit (RS) row, work even in St st until piece measures 1½"/4cm from beg, end with a WS row.
NEXT (DEC) ROW (RS) K4, *k2tog; rep from * to last 4 sts, k4—58 sts. Cont in St st until piece measures 3"/7.5cm from beg, end with a WS row. Place markers at each end of last row. Break yarn and leave sts on spare needle.

SECOND RUFFLE

With B, cast on 108 sts. Knit 1 (WS) row. Starting with a knit (RS) row, work even in St st until piece measures 1½"/4cm from beg, end with a WS row.
NEXT (DEC) ROW (RS) K4, *k2tog; rep from * to last 4 sts, k4—58 sts. Purl next row, placing markers at each end of last row.
NEXT (JOINING) ROW (RS) With RS facing and B, hold sts of second ruffle in front of those of first ruffle and, using 3-needle join, knit across—58 sts.
With B, cont in St st until second ruffle measures 3"/7.5cm from cast-on edge, end with a WS row.

THIRD RUFFLE

With C, cast on 108 sts. Knit 1 (WS) row. Starting with a knit (RS) row, work even in St st until piece measures 1½"/4cm from beg, end with a WS row.
NEXT (DEC) ROW (RS) K4, *k2tog; rep from * to last 4 sts, k4—58 sts. Purl next row.
NEXT (JOINING) ROW (RS) With RS facing and C, hold sts of third ruffle in front of those of second ruffle and, using 3-needle join, knit across—58 sts.
Purl next row.
Work in k1, p1 rib for ½"/1cm, end with a WS row. Bind off all sts in rib.

FINISHING

Sew back seam of first ruffle to markers. Sew back seam of second ruffle to markers. Sew snap to rib waist.

TOP
BODY

With A, cast on 53 sts. Knit 3 rows. Break A and join B. Starting with a knit (RS) row, work in St st until piece measures 2½"/6.5cm from beg, end with a WS row.

DIVIDE FOR FRONT AND BACKS

NEXT ROW (RS) K11, place last 11 sts worked on holder for left back, bind off next 3 sts for left armhole, knit until there are 25 sts on needle, place these sts on holder for front, bind off next 3 sts for right armhole, k11 for right back.

RIGHT BACK

NEXT ROW (WS) Purl—11 sts. Work even in St st until armhole measures 2½"/6.5cm, end with a WS row. Bind off.

LEFT BACK

Place 11 sts from left back holder on needle, ready for a WS row.
NEXT ROW (WS) Purl. Work even in St st until armhole measures 2½"/6.5cm, end with a WS row. Bind off.

FRONT

Place 25 sts from front holder on needle, ready for a WS row.
NEXT ROW (WS) Purl. Work even in St st until armhole measures 2"/5cm, end with a WS row.

NECK SHAPING

NEXT ROW (RS) K10, join a 2nd ball of yarn and bind off center 5 sts, k10. Working both sides at once, dec 1 st at each neck edge every row twice—8 sts rem each side for shoulder. Cont even in St st until armhole measures 2½"/6.5cm, end with a WS row. Bind off rem sts each side for shoulder.

SLEEVES

With B, cast on 23 sts. Knit 3 rows. Break B and join A. Starting with a knit (RS) row, work in St st until piece measures 1½"/4cm from beg, end with a WS row.

CAP SHAPING

Bind off 3 sts at beg of next 2 rows—17 sts.
NEXT ROW (RS) Change to A, cont in St st for ¾"/2cm. BO 3 sts at beg of next 2 rows—17 sts. Work even in St st for 6 rows, end with a WS row. Dec 1 st each end of every RS row 5 times—7 sts. Bind off.

FINISHING

Sew shoulder seams. Sew sleeve seams. Set in sleeves.

LEFT BACK BAND

With RS facing and B, starting at neck edge, pick up and k 36 sts evenly along left center back edge to cast-on. Work in k1, p1 rib for 3 rows. Bind off in rib.

RIGHT BACK BAND

Work as given for left back band, starting at cast-on edge and ending at neck edge.

NECKBAND

With RS facing and A, pick up and k 38 sts evenly around neck opening, including back bands. Knit 3 rows. Bind off all sts knitwise.
Mark position for 4 snaps, placing the first snap ½"/1cm down from neck edge, the last ½"/1cm up from lower edge, and the remaining 2 spaced evenly between. Sew one half of snap to WS of right back band at markers and the remaining half to RS of left back band.

ROSES
(MAKE 1 IN B, 1 IN A)
Loosely cast on 22 sts. Knit 1 row. Pass rem sts over last st and off the needle. Fasten off. Twist to shape into a rose.
Using photo as a guide, embroider stem and leaves to front using a running stitch. Sew roses to top of each stem, using photo as a guide.

BASKET

FRONT

With A, cast on 15 sts. Knit 3 rows. Break A and join C. Starting with a knit (RS) row, work in St st, decreasing 1 st at each end of 5th and every following 4th row twice—9 sts. Work even in St st until piece measures 2¾"/7cm, end with a WS row. Leave sts on holder.

BACK

Work as given for front. Using kitchener stitch, graft 9 sts from front to 9 sts from back. Sew side seams.

ROSES
(MAKE 1 IN A, 2 IN B)

Loosely cast on 22 sts. Knit 1 row. Pass rem sts over last st and off the needle. Fasten off. Twist to shape into a rose. With green, make loop leaves as shown and attach to underside of roses.

HANDLE (MAKE 2)

With crochet hook and C, ch 20. Fasten off. Attach to top of bag, using photo as a guide.

EMBROIDERY

With A, work couching embroidery st on front of bag. Sew roses to top of bag.✿

A candy-colored carrier for all her tiny treasures!

A Walk in the Woods

A dress with rustic texture goes girly with floral buttons in a pretty purple.

MATERIALS

- 1 3½oz/100g skein (each approx 438yd/400m) of Lion Brand *Sock Ease* (wool/nylon) in #138 grape soda

- One pair size 2 (2.75mm) needles, OR SIZE TO OBTAIN GAUGE

- One size 2 (2.75mm) circular needle, 16"/40cm long

- Cable needle (cn)

- Stitch markers and holders

- 3 decorative buttons

GAUGE

30 sts and 40 rows to 4"/10cm in St st using size 2 (2.75mm) needles. *Take time to check gauge.*

STITCH GLOSSARY

3-ST LC Sl 2 sts to cn and hold in *front*, k1, k2 from cn.

3-ST RC Sl 1 st to cn and hold in *back*, k2, k1 from cn.

4-ST LC Sl 2 sts to cn and hold in *front*, k2, k2 from cn.

4-ST RC Sl 2 sts to cn and hold in *back*, k2, k2 from cn.

K1, P1 RIB
(over an odd number of sts)
ROW 1 (RS) *K1, p1; rep from * to last st, k1.
ROW 2 P1, *k1, p1; rep from * to end.
Rep rows 1–2 for k1, p1 rib.

K2, P2 RIB
(over multiple of 4 sts plus 2)
ROW 1 (RS) *K2, p2; rep from * to last 2 sts, k2.
ROW 2 P2, *k2, p2; rep from * to end.
Rep rows 1–2 for k2, p2 rib.

K2, P2 RIB
(over multiple of 4 sts)
ROW 1 (RS) *K2, p2; rep from * to end.
ROW 2 *K2, p2; rep from * to end.
Rep rows 1–2 for k2, p2 rib.

BOX STITCH PATTERN
(over multiple of 4 sts plus 2)
ROW 1 (RS) P2, *k2, p2; rep from * to end.
ROWS 2 AND 3 K2, *p2, k2; rep from * to end.
ROW 4 P2, *k2, p2; rep from * to end.
Rep rows 1–4 for box st pat.

CABLE PATTERN A
(over 4 sts)
ROW 1 (RS) 4-st RC.
ROWS 2 AND 4 P4.
ROWS 3 AND 5 K4.
ROW 6 P4.
Rep rows 1–6 for cable pat A.

CABLE PATTERN B
(over 10 sts)
ROW 1 (RS) P3, 4-st LC, p3.
ROW 2 K3, p4, k3.
ROW 3 P2, 3-st RC, 3-st LC, p2.
ROW 4 K2, p6, k2.
ROW 5 P1, 3-st RC, k2, 3-st LC, p1.
ROW 6 K1, p8, k1.
ROW 7 3-st RC, k4, 3-st LC.
ROW 8 P10.
Rep rows 1–8 for cable pat B.

BACK

Cast on 54 sts. Work in k2, p2 rib for 5 rows, end with a RS row. Starting with row 1, work in box stitch pat until piece measures 6½"/16.5cm from beg, end with a WS row.

NEXT (DEC) ROW (RS) Work 26 sts in pat, k2tog, cont in pat to end of row—53 sts.

Starting with row 2, work in k1, p1 rib for 5 rows, increasing 1 st at center of last row—54 sts.

BEG CABLE PATS

NEXT ROW (RS) P2, work row 1 of cable pat A over next 4 sts, p1, work row 1 of cable pat B over next 10 sts, p2, [work row 1 of cable pat A over next 4 sts, p2] 3 times, work row 1 of cable pat B over next 10 sts, p1, work row 1 of cable pat A over next 4 sts, p2.

Cont in pat as established, working appropriate row of each cable, until piece measures 10"/25.5cm from beg, end with a WS row.

Slip sts to separate holders as follows: 18 for left shoulder, 18 for back neck, and 18 for right shoulder.

FRONT

Cast on 54 sts. Work in k2, p2 rib for 5 rows, end with a RS row. Starting with row 1, work in box stitch pat until piece measures 6½"/16.5cm from beg, end with a WS row.

NEXT (DEC) ROW (RS) Pat 26 sts, k2tog, pat to end of row—53 sts.

Starting with row 2, work in k1, p1 rib for 5 rows, end with a WS row.

BEG CABLE PATS AND DIVIDE FOR NECK OPENING

NEXT ROW (RS) P2, work row 1 of cable pat A over next 4 sts, p1, work row 1 of cable pat B over next 10 sts, p9, join a 2nd ball of yarn and bind off center st, p9, work row 1 of cable pat B over next 4 sts, p1, work row 1 of cable pat A over next 4 sts, p2—26 sts each side. Working both sides at once, cont in pat, decreasing 1 st at each neck edge every other row twice, then every 4th row 6 times—18 sts rem each side for shoulder. Work even until piece measures same as back. Place rem sts on holders for shoulder.

FINISHING

Using 3-needle bind-off, join 18 sts of back to front on each side. Place markers 2½"/6.5cm down from each shoulder on side edge of front and back for armholes.

ARMBANDS

With RS facing, pick up and k 38 sts between armhole markers. Starting with row 2, work in k2, p2 rib for 5 rows, end with a WS row. Bind off in rib.

NECKBAND

With circular needle and RS facing, pick up and k 24 sts up right front neck edge, k18 from back holder, pick up and k 24 sts down left front neck edge—66 sts. Turn and work back and forth in rows. Starting with row 2, work in k2, p2 rib for 5 rows, end with a WS row.

Beg short row shaping as foll: *Work in rib to last 4 sts, turn, work in rib to last 4 sts, turn. Rep from * 5 more times, leaving 4 more sts unworked each time (24 unworked sts each end on last rep). Turn and work in rib to end of row. Bind off all sts in rib.

POCKETS (MAKE 2)

Cast on 10 sts. Starting with row 1, work in box stitch pat for 16 rows, inc 1 st each end of 4th and 6th row, bringing inc sts into pat—14 sts.

NEXT ROW (RS) [P1, k1] 3 times, p2tog, [k1, p1] 3 times—13 sts. Work another 3 rows in k1, p1 rib, end with a WS row. Bind off in rib.

Sew pockets to front, following photo. Sew side and armband seams. Sew one button to center front and top edge of each pocket, centering in k1, p1 rib band.

HEADBAND

Cast on 96 sts. Work in k2, p2 rib for 1½"/4cm. Bind off in rib. Sew cast-on edge to bound-off edge.

WRISTLET (MAKE 2)

Cast on 32 sts. Work in k2, p2 rib for 1½"/4cm. Bind off in rib. Sew cast-on edge to bound-off edge.✿

Petite Parisienne

A chic poncho, a chapeau, and wristlets are the perfect accessories for a trip to the City of Light!

MATERIALS

- 1 1¾oz/50g skein (each approx 195yd/178m) of Crystal Palace *Mini Mochi* (wool) in #316 equinox
- One pair size 6 (4mm) needles, OR SIZE TO OBTAIN GAUGE
- 1 small snap
- 3 buttons (JHB/Nicky Epstein buttons #92744 Aldi used in sample)

GAUGE

24 sts and 44 rows to 4"/10cm over garter st using size 6 (4mm) needles. *Take time to check gauge.*

ROTATE PATTERN

(worked in short rows)

ROW 1 (RS) K3, turn; leaving 21 sts unworked.

ROW 2 AND ALL WS ROWS Knit.

ROW 3 K6, turn; leaving 18 sts unworked.

ROW 5 K9, turn; leaving 15 sts unworked.

ROW 7 K12, turn; leaving 12 sts unworked.

ROW 9 K15, turn; leaving 9 sts unworked.

ROW 11 K18, turn; leaving 6 sts unworked.

ROW 13 K21, turn; leaving 3 sts unworked.

ROW 15 Knit to end.

ROW 16 P3, k21.

Rep rows 1–16 for rotate pat.

PONCHO

Starting at left front center edge, cast on 24 sts. Knit 6 rows. Starting with row 1, work rows 1–16 of rotate pat 19 times, end with a WS row. Knit 6 rows. Bind off all sts knitwise.

FINISHING

Fold poncho in half so that center fronts meet. Measure 3"/7.5cm out from each side along bottom edge. Sew a ¾"/2cm seam at each of these points, beginning at bottom edge, to create sleeve. Sew front to back for 1¼"/3cm to shape sleeve. Sew buttons to left front edge, placing the first at neck edge, the last 1"/2.5cm from lower edge, and the remaining button halfway between. Sew half of snap to WS of left front at neck edge under button and the remaining half to right front.

HAT

Starting at center back, cast on 24 sts. Knit 2 rows. Starting with row 1, work rows 1–16 of rotate pat 9 times, end with a WS row. Bind off all sts knitwise.
Sew back seam. Gather top edge to close.

MITT (MAKE 2)
Cast on 12 sts. Work in garter st for 3"/7.5cm. Bind off knitwise.
Sew cast-on and bound-off edges together. Lay flat and tack front and back together along top edge, approx ½"/1.5cm in from folded edge, to create thumb opening. ✿

A simple circular pattern makes a pretty poncho.

Perfect Match

With this sporty hoodie, leggings, and headband, she's ready to hit the courts!

JACKET
BODY
With A, cast on 97 sts. Knit 6 rows, end with a WS row. Starting with a knit (RS) row, work in St st until piece measures 3"/7.5cm from beg, end with a WS row.
DEC ROW (RS) K1, [k2tog] 24 times, k1 [k2tog] 23 times, k1—50 sts. Work even in St st until piece measures 5"/12.5cm from beg, end with a WS row.

DIVIDE FOR FRONTS AND BACK
ROW 1 (RS) K11, place these 11 sts on holder for right front, bind off next 4 sts for right armhole, knit until there are 20 sts on needle, place these sts on holder for back, bind off next 4 sts for left armhole, k11 for left front.

LEFT FRONT
Starting with a purl (WS) row, work even in St st for 12 rows, end with a RS row.

NECK SHAPING
ROW 13 (WS) Bind off 3 sts, purl to end of row—8 sts. Work even until armhole measures 2"/5cm, end with a WS row. Bind off rem sts for shoulder.

BACK
Place 20 sts from back holder on needle, ready for a WS row.
ROW 1 (WS) Purl. Work even in St st until armhole measures 2"/5cm, end with a WS row. Bind off all sts.

RIGHT FRONT
Place 11 sts from right front holder on needle, ready for a WS row.
ROW 1 (WS) Purl. Work even in St st for 10 rows more, end with a WS row.

NECK SHAPING
ROW 12 (RS) Bind off 3 sts, purl to end of row—8 sts. Work even until armhole measures 2"/5cm,

end with a WS row. Bind off rem sts for shoulder.

SLEEVES

With A, cast on 21 sts. Knit 6 rows. Starting with a knit (RS) row, work in St st, inc 1 st each end of 5th and every following 6th row twice—27 sts.
Work even until piece measures 4½"/11.5cm from beg, end with a WS row.

CAP SHAPING

Bind off 3 sts at beg of next 2 rows—21 sts. Work 4 rows even. Dec 1 st at each end of next and every RS row 6 times more—7 sts. Bind off rem sts.

FINISHING

Sew shoulder seams. Sew sleeve seams. Set in sleeves.

HOOD

With RS facing and A, pick up and k 38 sts evenly around neck edge. Starting with a purl (WS) row, work in St st for 2"/5cm. Break A and join B. Cont even in St st until hood measures 5"/12.5cm from pickup row, end with a WS row.
NEXT ROW (RS) K19, then fold hood in half with RS together. Join top-of-hood seam using 3-needle bind-off.

FRONT TIES

With crochet hook and B, join yarn with a slip stitch at front waist (dec row) and work a ch for 4½"/11.5cm. Fasten off. Knot end. Rep on opposite side.

FRONT EDGING

With RS facing and B, starting at lower right front edge, pick up and k 150 sts evenly along front edges, including hood. Knit 5 rows, end with a WS row. Bind off all sts knitwise.

SHORTS
LEGS (MAKE 2)

With B, cast on 28 sts. Knit 4 rows. Starting with a knit (RS) row, work in St st until piece measures 2½"/6.5cm from beg, end with a WS row.

CROTCH SHAPING

ROW 1 (RS) K1, M1, knit to last st, M1, k1—30 sts. Work 1 row even.
Cast on 2 sts at beg of next 2 rows—34 sts. Cont in St st, dec 1 st at each end of 5th and every following 6th row twice more—28 sts. Work even until piece measures 6"/15cm from beg, end with a RS row. Knit 3 rows. Bind off all sts knitwise.

FINISHING

Sew leg inseams. Sew crotch/center back and front seam.

HEADBAND

With B, cast on 62 sts. Knit 6 rows. Bind off all sts knitwise. Sew cast-on and bound-off edges together. ✿

A Rose Is a Rose

A hat, clutch, and coat adorned with tiny sequins
and satin roses are the height of luxury.

MATERIALS
- 2 1¾oz/50g skeins (each approx 191yd/175m) of Rozetti *Polaris* (acrylic/Payette/wool) in #71005 scorpio
- One pair size 3 (3.25mm) needles, OR SIZE TO OBTAIN GAUGE
- One set (5) size 3 (3.25mm) dpn (double-pointed needles)
- Stitch markers and holders
- 5"/12.5cm velvet or satin ribbon, ¼"/64mm wide
- 3 small snaps
- 4 purchased ribbon roses

GAUGE
24 sts and 32 rows to 4"/10cm over St st using size 3 (3.25mm) needles. *Take time to check gauge.*

K1, P1 RIB
(over an odd number of sts)
ROW 1 (RS) *K1, p1; rep from * to last st, k1.
ROW 2 P1, *k1, p1; rep from * to end.
Rep rows 1–2 for k1, p1 rib.

3-NEEDLE JOIN
With RS of ruffles facing and the needles parallel, insert a third needle into the first st on each needle and knit the two stitches together.

NOTE
Body is made in one piece to armhole.

COAT
FIRST RUFFLE
Cast on 106 sts. Work 3 rows in garter st (knit every row), end with a WS row. Starting with a knit (RS) row, work in St st until piece measures 2"/5cm from beg, end with a WS row.
NEXT (DEC) ROW (RS)
K4, [k2tog] 49 times, k4—57 sts. Break yarn and leave sts on spare needle.

SECOND RUFFLE
Cast on 106 sts. Work 3 rows in garter st (knit every row), end with a WS row. Starting with a knit (RS) row, work in St st until piece measures 2"/5cm from beg, end with a WS row.
NEXT (DEC) ROW (RS)
K4, [k2tog] 49 times, k4—57 sts. Placing marker at each end of first row, work in St st until piece measures 3½"/9cm from beg, end with a WS row.
NEXT (JOINING) ROW (RS)
With first ruffle behind second ruffle, join ruffles together using 3-needle join—57 sts. Work a further 3½"/9cm in St st, end with a WS row.

DIVIDE FOR FRONTS AND BACK
NEXT ROW (RS)
K14, place these 14 sts worked onto holder for right front, bind off next 3 sts for right armhole, knit until there are 23 sts on needle, place these sts onto holder for back, bind off next 3 sts for left armhole, k14.

LEFT FRONT

Work even in St st until armhole measures 1½"/4cm, end with a RS row.

NECK SHAPING

NEXT ROW (WS) Bind off 4 sts, purl to end of row.

NEXT ROW Knit to last 3 sts, k2tog, k1—9 sts. Work even until armhole measures 2½"/6.5cm, end with a WS row. Bind off rem sts.

RIGHT FRONT

Place 14 sts from right front holder on needle, ready for a WS row.

NEXT ROW (WS)
Join yarn and purl to end of row. Cont even in St st until armhole measures 1½"/4cm, end with a WS row.

NECK SHAPING

NEXT ROW (RS) Bind off 4 sts, knit to end of row. Work 1 row even.

NEXT ROW (RS) K1, skp, knit to end of row—9 sts. Work even until armhole measures 2½"/6.5cm, end with a WS row. Bind off rem sts.

BACK

Place 23 sts from back holder on needle, ready for a WS row.

NEXT ROW (WS) Join yarn and purl to end of row. Cont even in St st until armhole measures 2½"/6.5cm, end with a WS row. Bind off all sts.

SLEEVES

Cast on 20 sts. Work 3 rows in garter st (knit every row), end with a WS row. Starting with a knit (RS) row, work in St st, increasing 1 st at each end of 5th row and every following 6th row twice—26 sts. Work even until piece measures 4"/10cm from beg, end with a WS row.

CAP SHAPING

Bind off 3 sts at beg of next 2 rows—20 sts. Work even in St st for 2"/5cm, end with a WS row. Bind off 2 sts at beg of next 2 rows—16 sts.

NEXT ROW (RS) *K2tog; rep from * to end—8 sts. Bind off rem sts.

FINISHING

Sew shoulder seams.

COLLAR

With RS facing, pick up and k 41 sts evenly around neck opening. Work in k1, p1 rib for 1½"/4cm. Bind off in rib.

RIGHT FRONT BAND

With RS facing, beg at marker, pick up and k 41 sts evenly along right front edge to start of neck shaping. Work in k1, p1 rib for ¾"/2cm. Bind off in rib.

LEFT FRONT BAND

With RS facing, beg at start of neck shaping, pick up and k 41 sts evenly along left front edge to marker. Work in k1, p1 rib for ¾"/2cm. Bind off in rib.
Sew ribbon roses to right front

band, placing the first ½"/1.5cm down from start of neck shaping, the last positioned in line with ruffle-join row, and the remainder spaced evenly between. Sew snaps to WS of right front band and RS of left front band to correspond to position of ribbon roses.
Sew sleeve seams. Set in sleeves, gathering bound-off edge to fit armhole opening.

HAT

Cast on 72 sts. Knit 1 (WS) row. Starting with a knit (RS) row, work in St st for 3½"/9cm, end with a WS row.

NEXT ROW (RS) *K3tog; rep from * to end—24 sts.

NEXT ROW *P3tog; rep from * to end—8 sts.
Cut yarn, leaving a long tail. Thread tail through rem sts. Draw up and secure. Sew center back seam.

I-CORD TRIM

With dpns and 2 strands held tog, cast on 5 sts. *Knit one row. Without turning work, slip sts back to beg of row. Pull yarn tightly from end of row. Rep from * until I-cord measures 24"/61cm. Bind off knitwise.

FINISHING

Fold cord in half and pin center point to back seam. Pin 4"/10cm of cord along cast-on edge, each side of back seam. Twist ends of cord twice, following photo. Pin in place. Slip stitch I-cord to hat from WS. Sew ribbon rose in position, using photo as a guide.

BAG

With 2 strands held tog, cast on 18 sts. Knit 1 (WS) row. Starting with a knit (RS) row, work in St st for 3½"/9cm, ending with a RS row. Knit 1 row. Bind off all sts purlwise.

FINISHING

With WS together, fold bag in half. Sew side seams. Sew snap to center top.

BOW

With 2 strands held tog, cast on 7 sts. Work in k1, p1 rib for 2½"/6.5cm. Bind off in rib. Cut 1"/2.5cm of ribbon and sew around center of bow tightly, forming small gathers at center. Fold and sew remaining 4"/10cm of ribbon to WS of bag at side seam for handle. Sew bow to center front of bag, using photo as a guide. ✿

All That Glitters

Lace, ribbon, and roses make a party gown for a princess—complete with a robe and golden crown.

MATERIALS

- 2 1¾oz/50g skeins (each approx 345yd/316m) of Tilli Tomas *Symphony Lace* (mohair/silk/nylon/wool) in natural with gold beads (MC)
- 1 0.88oz/25g skein (each approx 131yd/120m) of Filatura di Crosa *New Smoking* (viscose/polyester) in #01 gold (A)
- One pair size 3 (3.25mm) needles and one size 3 dpn, OR SIZE TO OBTAIN GAUGE
- One pair size 5 (3.75mm) needles
- Size D-3 (3.25mm) crochet hook
- Stitch markers and holders
- 3 gold ribbon roses
- 3 small snaps
- 1½yd/1.5m of ribbon, ¼"/60mm wide

GAUGE

26 sts and 38 rows to 4"/10cm over St st using size 3 (3.25mm) needles and MC. *Take time to check gauge.*

K1, P1 RIB

(over an odd number of sts)

ROW 1 (RS) *K1, p1; rep from * to last st, k1.

ROW 2 P1, *k1, p1; rep from * to end.

Rep rows 1–2 for k1, p1 rib.

3-NEEDLE JOIN

With RS of layers facing and the needles parallel, insert a third needle into the first st on each needle and purl the two sts together.

LACE PATTERN

(over multiple of 10 sts plus 3)

ROW 1 (RS) K2, *yo, k3, SK2P, k3, yo, k1; rep from * to last st, k1.

ROW 2 Purl.

ROW 3 K1, p1, *k1, yo, k2, SK2P, k2, yo, k1, p1; rep from * to last st, k1.

ROWS 4 AND 6 P1, *k1, p9; rep from * to last 2 sts, k1, p1.

ROW 5 K1, p1, *k2, yo, k1, SK2P, k1, yo, k2, p1; rep from * to last st, k1.

ROW 7 K1, p1, *k3, yo, SK2P, yo, k3, p1; rep from * to last st, k1.

ROW 8 Purl.

Rep rows 1–8 for lace pat.

NOTE

Body is made in one piece to armhole.

DRESS

FIRST LAYER

With larger needles, cast on 103 sts. Purl 1 (WS) row. Work rows 1–8 of lace pat 3 times, end with a WS row.

NEXT ROW (RS) K2, *k4, k2tog, k4; rep from * to last st, k1—93 sts. Break yarn, leaving sts on spare needle.

SECOND LAYER

With size 5 (3.75mm) needles, cast on 93 sts. Purl 1 (WS) row. Starting with row 1, work rows 1–7 of lace pat, end with a RS row.

NEXT (JOINING) ROW (WS) With WS facing, hold sts of second layer behind those of first layer and, using 3-needle join, purl across—93 sts.

Work rows 1–8 of lace pat twice more, end with a WS row.

NEXT (DEC) ROW (RS) K7, k2tog, [k7, k2tog, k6, k2tog] 4 times, k7, k2tog, k7—83 sts. Break yarn, leaving sts on spare needle.

THIRD LAYER

With size 5 (3.75mm) needles, cast on 83 sts. Purl 1 (WS) row. Work rows 1–7 of lace pat, end with a RS row.

NEXT (JOINING) ROW (WS) With WS facing, hold sts of third layer behind those of second layer and, using 3-needle join, purl across—83 sts.

Work rows 1–8 of lace pat twice more, end with a WS row. Place markers at each end of last row worked.

BODICE

Change to smaller needles.

ROW 1 (RS) Cast on 2 sts, sl 1, k39, k2tog, k40, k1—84 sts.

ROW 2 Cast on 2 sts, purl to end of row—86 sts.

ROW 3 K2, sl 1, knit to last 3 sts, sl 1, k2.

ROW 4 Purl.

Rep last 2 rows 5 times more, end with a WS row.

DIVIDE FOR FRONTS AND BACK

NEXT ROW (RS) K2, sl 1, k17, place last 20 sts worked on holder for left back, bind off next 6 sts for left armhole, knit until there are 34 sts on needle, place these sts on holder for back, bind off next 6 sts for right armhole, k17, sl 1, k2.

RIGHT BACK

NEXT ROW (WS) Purl—20 sts.

ROW 1 (RS) K2tog, k15, sl 1, k2—19 sts.

ROW 2 AND ALL WS ROWS Purl.

ROW 3 K2tog, k14, sl 1, k2—18 sts.

ROW 5 K15, sl 1, k2.

ROW 6 Purl.

Rep last 2 rows until armhole measures 2½"/6.5cm, end with a WS row. Place sts on holder for shoulder and back neck.

LEFT BACK

Place 20 sts from left back holder on needle, ready for a WS row.

NEXT ROW (WS) Purl—20 sts.

ROW 1 (RS) K2, sl 1, k15, k2tog—19 sts.

ROW 2 AND ALL WS ROWS Purl.

ROW 3 K2, sl 1, k14, k2tog—18 sts.

ROW 5 K2, sl 1, k15.

ROW 6 Purl.

Rep last 2 rows until armhole measures 2½"/6.5cm, end with a WS row. Place sts on holder for shoulder and back neck.

FRONT

Place 34 sts from front stitch holder on needle, ready for a WS row.

NEXT ROW (WS) Purl.

ROW 1 K2tog, knit to last 2 sts, k2tog—32 sts.

ROW 2 Purl.

Rep last 2 rows once more—30 sts. Work 4 rows even in St st, end with a WS row.

NECK SHAPING

NEXT ROW (RS) K11, place center 8 sts on holder, join a second ball of yarn and k11. Working both sides at once, dec 1 st at each neck edge every RS row 3 times—8 sts rem each side for shoulder. Work even in St st until armhole measures same as back, end with a WS row. Place rem 8 sts on each side on holders.

SLEEVES

With larger needles, cast on 33 sts. Purl 1 (WS) row. Work rows 1–6 of lace pat, end with a RS row. Change to smaller needles. Work in k1, p1 rib for 6 rows, end with a WS row. Change to larger needles. Work rows 1–8 of lace pat twice, end with a WS row.

CAP SHAPING

ROW 1 (RS) Bind off 3 sts, k3, ssk, k3, yo, k1, [yo, k3, sk2p, k3, yo, k1] twice, k1.

ROW 2 Bind off 3 sts, purl to end—27 sts.

ROW 3 K2tog, k1, ssk, k2, yo, k1, p1, k1, yo, k2, sk2p, k2, yo, k1, p1, k1, yo, k2, ssk, k1, k2tog—25 sts.

ROW 4 P7, k1, p9, k1, p7.

ROW 5 K2tog, ssk, k1, yo, k2, p1, k2, yo, k1, sk2p, k1, yo, k2, p1, k2, yo, k1, ssk, k2tog—23 sts.

ROW 6 P6, k1, p9, k1, p6.

ROW 7 K1, ssk, yo, k3, p1, k3, yo, sk2p, yo, k3, p1, k3, yo, ssk, k1.

ROWS 8, 10, 16, AND 18 Purl.

ROW 9 K1, ssk, k3, yo, k1, yo, k3, sk2p, k3, yo, k1, yo, k3, ssk, k1.

ROW 11 K1, ssk, k2, yo, k1, p1, k1, yo, k2, sk2p, k2, yo, k1, p1, k1, yo, k2, ssk, k1.

ROW 12 P6, k1, p9, k1, p6.

ROW 13 K1, ssk, k1, yo, k2, p1, k2, yo, k1, sk2p, k1, yo, k2, p1, k2, yo, k1, ssk, k1.

ROW 14 P6, k1, p9, k6, p1.

ROW 15 K1, ssk, yo, k3, p1, k3, yo, sk2p, yo, k3, p1, k3, yo, ssk, k1.

ROW 17 K1, [sk2p] 4 times, [k3tog] 3 times, k1—9 sts.

ROW 19 [Ssk] twice, k1, [k2tog] twice—5 sts.

ROW 20 Purl. Bind off all sts.

FINISHING

With 3-needle bind-off, join 8 shoulder sts of back to front on each side, leaving rem 10 sts each side of back on holder.

NECKBAND

With RS facing, sl first 2 sts on left back st holder to dpn and hold to back. With smaller needles, k1 (former sl st), 3-needle join next 2 sts to 2 sts on dpn (facing formed). Knit rem 5 left back sts, pick up and k 7 sts down left front neck edge, k8 from front holder, pick up and k 8 sts up right front neck edge, k5 from right back holder, 3-needle join next 2 sts to last 2 sts as for left side, k1 (former sl st)—38 sts.

NEXT ROW (WS) Purl. Bind off all sts knitwise.

Sew sleeve seams. Set in sleeves. Sew center back seam to markers, leaving overlap unsewn. Sew snaps to back bodice opening, placing the first snap at neck edge, the last 1"/2.5cm up from start of opening, and the remaining snap halfway between.

WRIST RIBBON

Cut two 7"/18cm lengths of ribbon. Place center of ribbon on underarm seam of sleeve at start of ribbing and slip st in place.

BODICE RIBBON

Cut a 26"/66cm length of ribbon. Measure 12"/30.5cm along one end and slip st under right underarm at start of bodice. Sew 3 ribbon roses to front neck, using photo as guide.

CROWN

With A, cast on 8 sts.

ROW 1 (RS) Knit.

ROW 2 Sl 1, k2, yo, k2tog, k1, [yo] 4 times, k2—12 sts.

ROW 3 Sl 1, k1, [k1, p1] twice into the 4 yo's, k3, yo, k2tog, k1.

ROW 4 Sl 1, k2, yo, k2tog, k7.

ROW 5 Sl 1, k8, yo, k2tog, k1.

ROW 6 Sl 1, k2, yo, k2tog, k7.

ROW 7 Bind off 4 sts, yo, k4, k2tog, k1—8 sts.

Rep rows 2–7 eighteen times more, end with a RS row. Bind off all sts purlwise.

Sew cast-on and bound-off edges together.

ROBE

With A, cast on 73 sts. Knit 1 (WS) row. Starting with a knit (RS) row, work 6 rows in St st, end with a WS row. Break A and join MC. Work even in St st for 2½"/6.5cm, end with a WS row. Break MC and join A. Work 6 rows in St st, end with a WS row. Break A and join MC. Work even in St st for 2¼"/6cm, end with a WS row. Break MC and join A. Work 6 rows in St st, end with a WS row. Break A and join MC. Work even in St st for 3"/7.5cm, end with a WS row.

NEXT (DEC) ROW (RS) With MC, k1, *k3tog; rep from * to end of row—25 sts. Break MC and join A.

NEXT ROW Purl.

Work in k1, p1 rib for 4 rows, end with a WS row.

ROW 1 (INC) (RS) K1, *p1, yo, k1; rep from * to end of row—37 sts.

ROW 2 *P1, k2, rep from * to last st, p1.

ROW 3 K1, *p2, yo, k1; rep from * to end of row—49 sts.

ROW 4 *P1, k3; rep from * to last st, p1.

ROW 5 K1, *p3, yo, k1; rep from * to end of row—61 sts.

ROW 6 *P1, k4; rep from * to last st, p1.

ROW 7 K1, *p4, yo, k1; rep from * to end of row—73 sts.

ROW 8 *P1, k5; rep from * to last st, p1.

ROW 9 K1, *p5, k1; rep from * to end of row. Bind off all sts in pat.

FINISHING

With crochet hook, RS facing, and A, work 1 row sc evenly along each center front edge. Fasten off. Lightly block.✿

Fairy-Tale Blanket

A sparkly blanket and matching pillow depict every little girl's fantasy: a castle to call her own.

FINISHED MEASUREMENTS

Afghan approx
15"/38cm x 16"/40.5cm

Pillow approx
7"/18cm x 4½"/11.5cm

MATERIALS

▪ 1 1¾oz/50g skein (each approx 157yd/144m) of Lion Brand *Vanna's Sequins* (acrylic/polyester) in #150 sterling

▪ One pair size 5 (3.75mm) needles, OR SIZE TO OBTAIN GAUGE

▪ Polyester fiberfill

▪ 7" x 4½" (18cm x 11.5cm) piece of felt

▪ Castle appliqué (optional)

GAUGE

20 sts and 28 rows to 4"/10cm over St st using size 5 (3.75mm) needles. *Take time to check gauge.*

SEED STITCH

(over an even number of sts)
ROW 1 (RS) *K1, p1; rep from * to end.
ROW 2 K the purl and p the knit sts.
Rep row 2 for seed st.

SEED STITCH

(over an odd number of sts)
ROW 1 (RS) K1, *p1, k1; rep from * to end.
ROW 2 K the purl and p the knit sts.
Rep row 2 for seed st.

AFGHAN

Cast on 72 sts. Work in seed st for 8 rows, end with a WS row.
NEXT ROW (RS) Work 6 sts in seed st, work row 1 of chart over next 60 sts, work last 6 sts in seed st.
Keeping first and last 6 sts in seed st, work chart to end (row 82), end with a WS row. Work in seed st over all sts for 8 rows. Bind off in pat.

FINISHING

TASSEL (MAKE 4)
Wrap yarn 30 times around a piece of scrap cardboard. For tassel ties, cast on 10 sts, knit 1 row. Bind off. Wrap tie around neck of tassel and secure. Sew tassel to each corner of afghan.

PILLOW

FRONT
Cast on 35 sts. Work in seed st for 6 rows, end with a WS row.
NEXT ROW (RS) Work 6 sts in seed st, k23, work last 6 sts in seed st.
NEXT ROW Work 6 sts in seed st, p23, work last 6 sts in seed st. Rep last 2 rows until piece measures 4¼"/11cm from beg, end with a WS row.
Work in seed st over all sts for 6 rows. Bind off in pat.

FINISHING

Sew front and felt backing together, leaving a small opening. Stuff pillow with polyester fiberfill. Sew opening closed. Sew appliqué in place, using photo as a guide. ✿

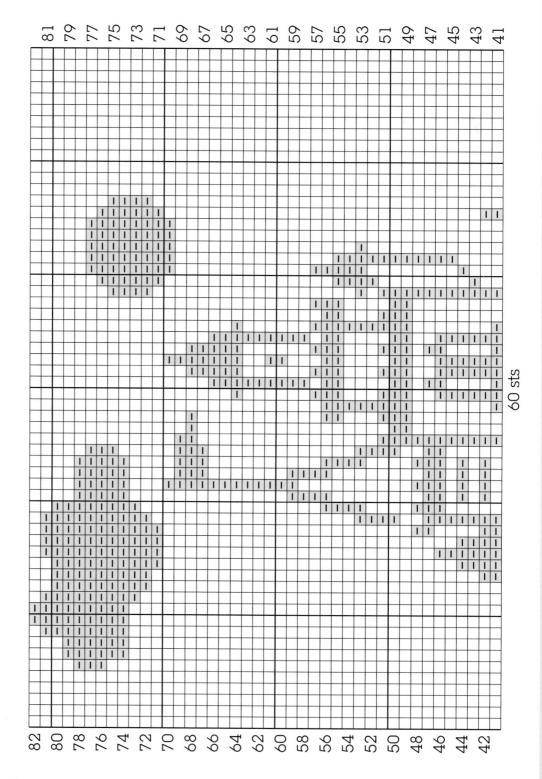

81 79 77 75 73 71 69 67 65 63 61 59 57 55 53 51 49 47 45 43 41

60 sts

STITCH KEY

☐ k on RS,
p on WS

⊟ p on RS,
k on WS

82 80 78 76 74 72 70 68 66 64 62 60 58 56 54 52 50 48 46 44 42

42

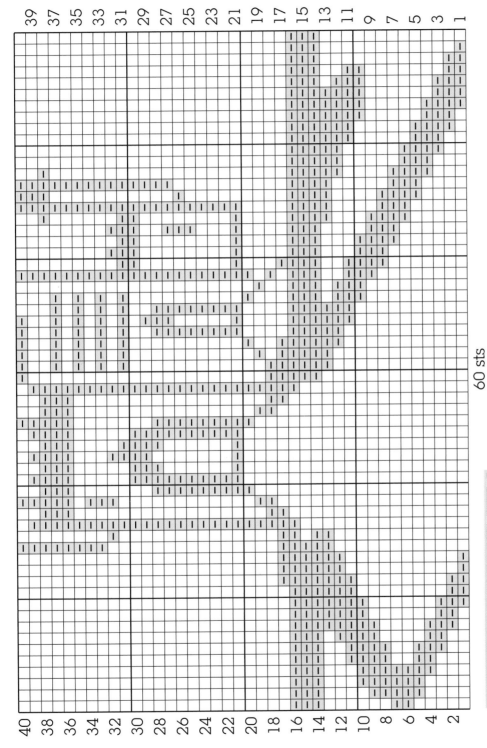

60 sts

Mirror, Mirror

A royal dressmaker could have created this beautifully beaded set in shades of purple fit for a princess.

MATERIALS

- 2 balls (each approx 300 yd/274m) of Aunt Lydia's *Bamboo Crochet Thread* (viscose from bamboo) in #536 lilac
- One pair size 0 (2mm) needles, OR SIZE TO OBTAIN GAUGE
- One size 0 (2mm) circular needle, 12"/30cm in length
- 1 hank Deanna's Vintage Style Beads, size 8, #596 Lavender
- Stitch markers and holders
- Velcro or small snaps
- Crochet hook and waste yarn for provisional cast-on
- 12"/30.5cm of ¼"/64mm elastic
- 8"/20.5cm of ⅛"/32mm ribbon

GAUGE

42 sts and 56 rows to 4"/10cm over St st using size 0 (2mm) needles. *Take time to check gauge.*

STITCH GLOSSARY

SB (slip bead) Bring the yarn and the bead to the front of the work and slip the next st knitwise. Bring the yarn to the back, keeping the bead to the front.

PB (place bead) Place bead between last st worked and next st on needle.

PROVISIONAL CAST-ON

With crochet hook and waste yarn, crochet a chain several sts longer than the required number of sts to be cast on. Fasten off. With knitting needle, pick up and knit the required number of sts in the bumps of the chain, leaving a couple of empty chains at either end. When instructed, "unzip" the sts by undoing the fastened-off end of the chain and pulling it out, placing the open sts on the knitting needle as you go.

NOTES

1) Top is worked in one piece to armhole.
2) Skirt is worked from the top down, in the round.
3) Knit (or purl) stitch after SB firmly.

TOP

Thread 370 beads onto yarn. With straight needles, cast on 100 sts.

ROWS 1, 3, AND 5 (RS) P2, *PB, p2; rep from * to end of row.

ROWS 2, 4, AND 6 K2, *PB, k2; rep from * to end of row, placing marker at beg of row 6.

ROWS 7 AND 9 Knit.

ROW 8 AND ALL WS ROWS Purl.

ROWS 11 AND 23 K42, SB, k14, SB, k42.

ROWS 13 AND 21 K41, SB, k1, SB, k12, SB, k1, SB, k41.

ROWS 15 AND 19 K40, SB, k3, SB, k10, SB, k3, SB, k40.

ROW 17 K39, SB, k5, SB, k8, SB, k5, SB, k39.

Rep rows 11–24 once more, then rows 11–16 once, end with a WS row.

DIVIDE FOR FRONT AND BACKS

NEXT ROW (RS) K23, place these 23 sts worked on holder for left back, bind off next 4 sts for left armhole, k12, SB, k5, SB, k8, SB, k5, SB, k12, place last 46 sts worked on holder for front, bind off next 4 sts for right armhole, k23 for right back.

RIGHT BACK
ROW 1 (WS) P23.
ROW 2 (RS) K2tog, knit to end of row.
Rep rows 1 and 2 twice more—20 sts. Work even in St st until armhole measures 2"/5cm, end with a WS row.

NECK SHAPING
NEXT ROW (RS) K12, turn and leave rem 8 sts on holder for neck—12 sts.
Cont even in St st until armhole measures 2½"/6.5cm, end with a WS row.

SHOULDER SHAPING
Bind off 4 sts at beg of next 3 RS rows.

LEFT BACK
Place 23 sts from left back holder on needle, ready for a WS row.
ROW 1 (WS) P23.
ROW 2 (RS) Knit to last 2 sts, k2tog.
Rep rows 1 and 2 twice more—20 sts. Work even in St st until armhole measures 2"/5cm, end with a RS row.

NECK SHAPING
NEXT ROW (WS) P12, turn and leave rem 8 sts on holder for neck—12 sts.
Cont even in St st until armhole measures 2½"/6.5cm, end with a RS row.

SHOULDER SHAPING
Bind off 4 sts at beg of next 3 WS rows.

FRONT
Place 46 sts from front holder on needle, ready for a WS row.
ROW 1 (WS) Purl.
ROW 2 (RS) K2tog, k11, SB, k3, SB, k10, SB, k3, SB, k11, k2tog—44 sts.
ROW 3 Purl.
ROW 4 K2tog, k11, SB, k1, SB, k12, SB, k1, SB, k11, k2tog—42 sts.
ROW 5 Purl.
ROW 6 K2tog, k11, SB, k14, SB, k11, k2tog—40 sts.
Cont even in St st until armhole measures 1¼"/3cm, end with a WS row.

NECK SHAPING
NEXT ROW (RS) K23, place last 6 sts worked on holder for front neck, k17. Working both sides at once, dec 1 st from each neck edge every RS row 5 times—12 sts rem each side for shoulder. Work even until armhole measures 2½"/6.5cm.

SHOULDER SHAPING
Bind off 4 sts at each shoulder edge 3 times.

SLEEVES
Thread 150 beads onto yarn. With straight needles, cast on 40 sts.
ROWS 1, 3, AND 5 (RS) P2, *PB, p2; rep from * to end of row.

ROWS 2, 4, AND 6 K2, *PB, k2; rep from * to end of row.
ROW 7 Knit, increasing 1 st at center of row—41 sts.

ROWS 8–12 Starting with a purl (WS) row, work in St st.
ROWS 13 AND 29 K20, SB, k20.
ROW 14 AND ALL WS ROWS Purl.
ROWS 15 AND 27 K19, SB, k1, SB, k19.
ROWS 17 AND 25 K18, SB, k3, SB, k18.
ROWS 19 AND 23 K17, SB, k5, SB, k17.
ROW 21 K16, SB, k7, SB, k16.
Rep rows 13–30 once more, end with a WS row.

CAP SHAPING
Bind off 2 sts at beg of next 2 rows. Dec 1 st at each end of next and every following RS row twice more, end with a WS row—31 sts. Bind off 3 sts at beg of next 2 rows, 4 sts at beg of next 4 rows—9 sts. Bind off rem 9 sts.

FINISHING
RIGHT BACK EXTENSION
With RS facing, starting at neck shaping, pick up and k 43 sts evenly along center right back edge to marker. Starting with a purl (WS) row, work 9 rows in St st, end with a WS row.
Bind off all sts.
Sew shoulder seams. Sew sleeve seams. Set in sleeves.

NECKBAND

Thread 320 beads onto yarn. With RS facing, k8 sts from left back holder, pick up and k 25 sts evenly along left neck edge to front holder, k6 sts from front holder, pick up and k 25 sts evenly along right neck edge to back holder, k8 sts from right back holder—72 sts.

ROW 1 P2, *PB, p2; rep from * to end of row.

ROW 2 K2, *PB, k2; rep from * to end of row.

Rep last 2 rows 3 times more, then row 1 once. Bind off all sts. Roll neckband to RS and slip stitch to neck edge.

Sew one half of snap to RS of right back extension, placing the first at start of neck shaping, the last 2½"/6.5cm down from neck shaping, and the remainder spaced evenly between. Place remaining half of snap to WS of left back to correspond.

SKIRT

Thread 1,345 beads onto yarn.

WAISTBAND CASING

With straight needles, cast on 125 sts using provisional cast-on. Starting with a knit (RS) row, work 10 rows in St st, end with a WS row.

Carefully remove waste yarn, placing the 125 sts on spare needle. Hold spare needle behind working needle with WS tog.

NEXT (JOINING) ROW (RS) With circular needle, *insert a third needle into the first st on each needle and knit the two sts together; rep from * to end of row—125 sts. Place marker for beg of rnd.

MAIN BODY OF SKIRT

RNDS 1–10 Knit.

RND 11 *SB, k24; rep from * to end of rnd.

RNDS 12, 14, 16, AND 18 Knit.

RND 13 *K1, SB, k22, SB; rep from * to end of rnd.

RND 15 *K2, SB, k20, SB, k1; rep from * to end of rnd.

RND 17 *K3, SB, k18, SB, k2; rep from * to end of rnd.

RND 19 *K4, SB, k1, m1, k6, SB, k1, SB, k5, m1, k1, SB, k3; rep from * to end of rnd—135 sts.

RND 20 AND ALL EVEN-NUMBERED RNDS Knit.

RNDS 21 AND 35 *K3, SB, k9, SB, k1, SB, k8, SB, k2; rep from * to end of rnd.

RNDS 23 AND 33 *K2, SB, k10, SB, k1, SB, k9, SB, k1; rep from * to end of rnd.

RNDS 25 AND 31 *K1, SB, k11, SB, k1, SB, k10, SB; rep from * to end of rnd.

RNDS 27 AND 29 *SB, k12, SB, k1, SB, k11; rep from * to end of rnd.

RND 37 *K4, SB, k1, m1, k7, SB, k1, SB, k6, m1, k1, SB, k3; rep from * to end of rnd—145 sts.

RNDS 39 AND 53 *K3, SB, k10, SB, k1, SB, k9, SB, k2; rep from * to end of rnd.

RNDS 41 AND 51 *K2, SB, k11, SB, k1, SB, k10, SB, k1; rep from * to end of rnd.

RNDS 43 AND 49 *K1, SB, k12, SB, k1, SB, k11, SB; rep from * to end of rnd.

RNDS 45 AND 47 *SB, k13, SB, k1, SB, k12; rep from * to end of rnd.

RND 55 *K4, SB, k1, m1, k8, SB, k1, SB, k7, m1, k1, SB, k3; rep from * to end of rnd—155 sts.

RNDS 57 AND 71 *K3, SB, k11, SB, k1, SB, k10, SB, k2; rep from * to end of rnd.

RNDS 59 AND 69 *K2, SB, k12, SB, k1, SB, k11, SB, k1; rep from * to end of rnd.

RNDS 61 AND 67 *K1, SB, k13, SB, k1, SB, k12, SB; rep from * to end of rnd.

RNDS 63 AND 65 *SB, k14, SB, k1, SB, k13; rep from * to end of rnd.

RND 73 *K4, SB, k1, m1, k9, SB, k1, SB, k8, m1, k1, SB, k3; rep from * to end of rnd—165 sts.

RNDS 75 AND 89 *K3, SB, k12, SB, k1, SB, k11, SB, k2; rep from * to end of rnd.

RNDS 77 AND 87 *K2, SB, k13, SB, k1, SB, k12, SB, k1; rep from * to end of rnd.

RNDS 79 AND 85 *K1, SB, k14, SB, k1, SB, k13, SB; rep from * to end of rnd.

RNDS 81 AND 83 *SB, k15, SB, k1, SB, k14; rep from * to end of rnd.

RND 91 *K4, SB, k1, m1, k10, SB, k1, SB, k9, m1, k1, SB, k3; rep from * to end of rnd—175 sts.
RND 93 *K3, SB, k13, SB, k1, SB, k12, SB, k2; rep from * to end of rnd.
RND 95 *K2, SB, k14, SB, k1, SB, k13, SB, k1; rep from * to end of rnd.
RND 97 *K1, SB, k15, SB, k1, SB, k14, SB; rep from * to end of rnd.

RND 99 *SB, k34; rep from * to end of rnd.
RND 100 Knit.
RNDS 101, 102, AND 103 P1, *SB, p1; rep from * to end of rnd. Bind off all sts purlwise.

FINISHING
Insert elastic into waistband casing and adjust to fit doll's waist. Sew ends of elastic together. Sew edges of casing together.

BAG
Thread 15 beads onto yarn. Cast on 32 sts. Starting with a knit (RS) row, work 4 rows in St st.
NEXT (EYELET) ROW (RS) K2, *yo, k2tog; rep from * to end of row.
Starting with a purl (WS) row, work 5 rows in St st, end with a WS row.
NEXT ROW (RS) K2, *PB, k2; rep from * to end of row.
Cont even in St st until piece measures 2"/5cm from beg, end with a WS row.
NEXT ROW (RS) *K2, k2tog; rep from * to end of row—24 sts. Draw yarn though rem sts, pull tight and secure. Sew center back seam.
Starting and ending at seam, thread ribbon through eyelet row. Knot ends of ribbon together.✿

Skullduggery

Bright pink adds a girlish touch to a tough-as-nails goth tunic.

MATERIALS

- 1 1¾ oz/50g skein (each approx 131yd/120m) of Filatura Di Crosa *Sportwool* (wool) each in #11 black (MC), #1 white (A), and #1357 pink (B)
- One pair size 3 (3.25mm) needles, OR SIZE TO OBTAIN GAUGE
- Stitch holders
- 2 small snaps

GAUGE

24 sts and 36 rows to 4"/10cm over St st using size 3 (3.25mm) needles. *Take time to check gauge.*

NOTE

Skull motif is worked in duplicate stitch.

FRONT

With MC, cast on 40 sts. Work in St st for 6 rows.

NEXT ROW (TURNING RIDGE) (RS) Purl.
NEXT ROW Purl.

BEG CHART 1

Starting and ending where indicated, work Chart 1 in St st to end of chart, end with a WS row. With MC, work even in St st until piece measures 7"/18cm from turning ridge, end with a WS row.

RAGLAN SHAPING

Bind off 2 sts at beg of next 2 rows—36 sts.
NEXT ROW (RS) K1, k2tog, knit to last 3 sts, ssk, k1—34 sts.
NEXT ROW Purl.
Rep last 2 rows 8 times more—18 sts.

NECK SHAPING

NEXT ROW (RS) Ssk, k3, join a 2nd ball of yarn and bind off center 8 sts, k3, ssk—4 sts each side. Working both sides at once, dec 1 st at neck and raglan edge on next RS row—2 sts. Work 1 row even. Leave rem 2 sts each side on holder.

BACK

Work as for front to raglan shaping.

RAGLAN SHAPING

Bind off 2 sts at beg of next 2 rows—36 sts.

NEXT ROW (RS) K1, k2tog, k15, join a 2nd ball of yarn and k15, ssk, k1—17 sts rem each side. Working each side at once, dec 1 st at raglan seam every RS row 10 times more, end with a WS row—7 sts rem each side. Place rem sts on holders.

SLEEVES

With B, cast on 24 sts. Work in k1, p1 rib for ¾"/2cm, end with a WS row. Break B and join MC. Starting and ending where indicated, work Chart 1 in St st to end of chart, inc 1 st at each end of 5th and every following 4th row twice—30 sts. With MC, work even in St st until piece measures 4"/10cm from beg, end with a WS row.

RAGLAN SHAPING

Bind off 2 sts at beg of next 2 rows—26 sts.
NEXT ROW (RS) K1, k2tog, knit to last 3 sts, ssk, k1—24 sts.
NEXT ROW Purl.
Rep last 2 rows 10 times—4 sts. Place rem 4 sts on holder.

CHART 2

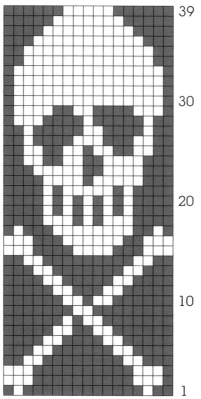

FINISHING

Block pieces. Sew raglan sleeve seams.

With A, work skull foll chart 2 using duplicate st, centering chart.
Sew side and sleeve seams.
Fold hem to WS along turning ridge and sew in place.

TURTLENECK

With RS facing and B, pick up and k 41 sts evenly around neck opening, including sts on holders.
Work k1, p1 rib for 2½"/6cm.
Bind off in rib.
Sew snaps to turtleneck, placing the first at bound-off edge and the second at turtleneck pickup row. ✿

17 sts

CHART 1

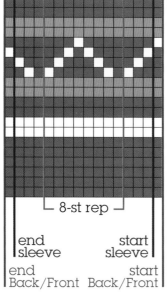

8-st rep

end sleeve   start sleeve

end Back/Front   start Back/Front

Modern Masterpiece

Striking Fair Isle motifs and vibrant stripes make this dress a work of art.

MATERIALS

- 1 2.8oz/80g 8-pack of skeins (each approx 38yd/35m) of Lion Brand *Bonbons* (acrylic/metallic polyester) in #660 celebrate
- One pair size 3 (3.25mm) needles, OR SIZE TO OBTAIN GAUGE
- Size D-3 (3.25mm) crochet hook
- Stitch markers and holders
- 4 snaps

GAUGE

24 sts and 36 rows to 4"/10cm over St st using size 3 (3.25mm) needles. *Take time to check gauge.*

K1, P1 RIB

(over an even number of sts)
ROW 1 (RS) *K1, p1; rep from * to end.
Rep row 1 for k1, p1 rib.

K1, P1 RIB

(over an odd number of sts)
ROW 1 (RS) *K1, p1; rep from * to last st, k1.
ROW 2 P1, *k1, p1; rep from * to end.
Rep rows 1–2 for k1, p1 rib.

NOTES

1) Use the following colors: emerald (A), pea green (B), dark blue (C), peach (D), light blue (E), purple (F). Remaining colors are not needed.
2) Dress is worked in one piece from bottom to yoke.
3) Yoke is worked back and forth in one piece to neck edge.

SLEEVES

With B, cast on 26 sts. Work in k1, p1 rib for 2¼"/5.5cm, end with a WS row. Break B and join A.
NEXT ROW (RS) With A, cont in rib, inc 1 st at each end of 5th and every following 4th row twice—32 sts. Cont even in rib until piece measures 4"/10cm, end with a WS row.

Bind off 3 sts at beg of next 2 rows—26 sts. Place sts on holder for yoke.

BODY

With A, cast on 79 sts. Work in k1, p1 rib for 4 rows, end with a WS row. Break A and join B.

BEG CHART PAT
NEXT ROW (RS) Starting and ending where indicated, work to end of chart, end with a RS row. Break E and join C.
ROW 1 (RS) K5, *p3, k4; rep from * to last 4 sts, p4.
ROW 2 K4, *p4, k3; rep from * to last 5 sts, p5.
Rep last 2 rows until piece measures 4½"/11.5cm, end with a WS row. Break C and join E.
NEXT ROW (RS) With E, knit. Starting with row 2, work in k1, p1 rib until piece measures 6"/15cm from beg, end with a WS row. Break E and join A.
NEXT ROW (RS) With A, knit. Work 2 rows in k1, p1 rib, placing markers at each end of last row worked.

DIVIDE FOR FRONT AND BACKS

NEXT ROW (WS) With A, work 18 sts in rib, bind off next 6 sts for right underarm, work 31 sts in rib, bind off next 6 sts for left underarm, work 18 sts in rib. Break A and join B.

YOKE

ROW 1 (RS) With B, k18 (left back), k26 from first sleeve, k31 (front) dec 1 st at center, k26 from second sleeve, k18 (right back)—118 sts.

ROW 2 Purl.

ROW 3 (RS) With B, work 4 sts in rib, *with F, k2, with B, k4; rep from * to last 6 sts, with F, k2, with B, work 4 sts in rib.

ROW 4 With B, rib 4, with F, p2, *with B, p4, with F, p2; rep from * to last 4 sts, with B, rib 4.

ROW 5 (RS) With B, rib 4, *with F, k2, with B, k1, k2tog, k1; rep from * to last 6 sts, with F, k2, with B, rib 4—100 sts.

ROW 6 With B, rib 4, with F, p2, *with B, p3, with F, p2; rep from * to last 4 sts, with B, rib 4. Break B.

ROW 7 (RS) With F, rib 4, knit to last 4 sts, rib 4.

ROW 8 With F, rib 4, purl to last 4 sts, rib 4. Break F and join D.

ROW 9 (RS) With D, rib 4, knit to last 4 sts, rib 4.

ROW 10 With D, rib 4, purl to last 4 sts, rib 4.

ROW 11 (RS) With D, rib 4, *with E, k3, with D, k3; rep from * to last 6 sts, with E, k2, with D, rib 4.

ROW 12 With D, rib 4, with E, k2, *with D, p3, with E, k3; rep from * to last 10 sts, with D, p3, with E, k3, with D, rib 4.

ROW 13 (RS) With D, rib 4, knit to last 4 sts, rib 4.

ROW 14 With D, rib 4, purl to last 4 sts, rib 4. Break D and join C.

ROW 15 (RS) With C, rib 4, k5, *k4, k2tog; rep from * to last 7 sts, k3, rib 4—86 sts.

ROW 16 With C, rib 4, purl to last 4 sts, rib 4.

ROW 17 (RS) With C, rib 4, *k2tog, k3; rep from * to last 7 sts, k3, rib 4—71 sts.

ROW 18 With C, rib 4, purl to last 4 sts, rib 4. Break C and join F.

ROW 19 (RS) With F, rib 4, k2, *k2tog, k2; rep from * to last 5 sts, k1, rib 4—56 sts.
Work 3 rows in k1, p1 rib, end with a WS row. Bind off in rib.

FINISHING

Sew center back seam from cast-on edge to markers. Sew sleeve and underarm seams. Sew 3 snaps to back opening, placing the first ¼"/0.5cm from neck edge, the last ½"/1.5cm from start of back opening, and the remainder spaced evenly between.

BAG

With D, cast on 23 sts.

Work 4 rows in garter st, end with a WS row. Join F.

ROW 1 (RS) With F, knit.

ROW 2 With F, purl.

ROW 3 *With D, k3, with F, k2; rep from * to last 3 sts, with D, k3.

ROW 4 *With D, p3, with F, p2; rep from * to last 3 sts, with D, p3.
Rep last 2 rows once more.
With D, work even in St st for 3½"/9cm, end with a WS row.

ROW 1 (RS) *With D, k3, with F, k2; rep from * to last 3 sts, with D, k3.

ROW 2 *With D, p3, with F, p2; rep from * to last 3 sts, with D, p3.
Rep last 2 rows once more.

ROWS 3 AND 4 Rep rows 1 and 2 once more.

ROW 5 (RS) With F, knit.

ROW 6 With F, purl. Break F.
With D, work 4 rows in garter st, end with a WS row.
Bind off all sts.

FINISHING

With WS together, fold bag in half and sew side seams.

HANDLE

With crochet hook and 2 strands of D, ch 45. Fasten off. Sew ends of handle to top edge of each side seam. Sew snap to inside front and back for closure.

HEADBAND

With E, cast on 17 sts. Work 8 rows in k1, p1 rib, end with a WS row. Break E and join B.

ROW 9 (RS) Knit.

ROWS 10–12 Starting with a WS row, work 3 rows in k1, p1 rib. Break B and join F.

ROW 13 (RS) Knit. Starting with a WS row, work in k1, p1 rib until piece measures 6"/15cm from beg, end with a WS row. Break F and join D.

ROW 1 (RS) Knit.

ROWS 2–4 Starting with a WS row, work 3 rows in k1, p1 rib. Break D and join A.

ROW 5 (RS) Knit.

ROWS 6–12 Starting with a WS row, work 7 rows in k1, p1 rib, end with a WS row. Bind off in rib.

FINISHING

Sew cast-on and bound-off edges together and gather seam. Pull tightly and secure.

TIE

With B, cast on 5 sts, work in rib for 2"/5cm. Bind off in rib. Wrap tie around center gather of band and sew cast-on and bound-off edges together to secure. ✿

STITCH KEY

☐ k on RS, p on WS
⊟ p on RS, k on WS

COLOR KEY

■ pea green (B)
■ peach (D)
■ light blue (E)
■ purple (F)

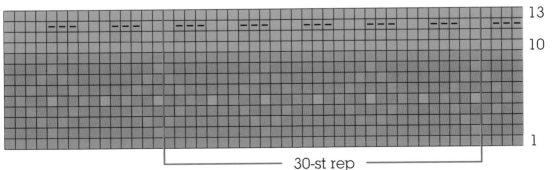

30-st rep

13
10
1

What a Hoot!

Make a knitted sundress airy and fun with whimsical fabric and an adorable owl on the bodice.

MATERIALS
- 1 1¾oz/50g skein (each approx 136yd/125m) of *Cascade Ultra Pima Fine* (cotton) in #3750 tangerine
- One pair size 3 (3.25mm) needles, OR SIZE TO OBTAIN GAUGE
- Stitch holders
- 2 small snaps
- Fabric, 21" wide x 13" long (53cm x 33cm)
- Sewing machine and thread
- Owl appliqué (optional)

GAUGE
22 sts and 30 rows to 4"/10cm over seed st using size 3 (3.25mm) needles. *Take time to check gauge.*

SEED STITCH
(over an even number of sts)
ROW 1 (RS) *K1, p1; rep from * to end.
ROW 2 *P1, k1; rep from * to end.
Rep row 2 for seed st.

NOTE
Skirt is made of fabric and sewn to bodice.

BODICE
Cast on 61 sts. Work in seed st for 14 rows, end with a WS row.
ROW 15 (RS) Bind off 22 sts, work 4 sts in pat and place on holder for left shoulder strap, bind off next 9 sts, work in pat for 4 sts and place on holder for right shoulder strap, bind off rem 22 sts.

SHOULDER STRAPS
Place 4 sts from right shoulder strap holder on needle, ready for a WS row. Work in pat for 3¾"/9.5cm. Bind off in pat. Rep for left shoulder strap. Sew bound-off edge of straps to back.

SKIRT
Fold lower edge of fabric over ¼"/0.5cm, then ¾"/2cm again to hem. With sewing machine, stitch the hem ⅝" from lower edge. Press.
Fold top edge of fabric over ¼"/0.5cm, then ½/1.5cm again to hem. With sewing machine, make 2 rows of running stitches through hem. Sew center back seam of skirt, leaving 2½"/6.5cm opening at upper edge. Pull upper hem to gather skirt to fit along cast-on edge of bodice. Slip stitch bodice to skirt, with gathered hem behind bodice.

FINISHING
Mark position for 2 snaps at back opening of top, placing the first at bound-off edge and the second at cast-on edge. Sew one half of snap to WS of left back at markers and the remaining half to RS of right back. If desired, sew appliqué in place at center front, using photo as a guide.

HAT
Cast on 71 sts. Work in seed st until piece measures 2"/5cm from beg, end with a WS row.

SHAPE CROWN
ROW 1 (RS) K1, *k2tog; rep from * to end of row—36 sts.
ROW 2 *P2tog; rep from * to end of row—18 sts.
ROW 3 *K2tog; rep from * to end of row—9 sts. Cut yarn, leaving a long tail. Thread tail through rem sts. Draw up and secure. Sew center back seam.

FLOWER
Cast on 50 sts. Starting with a knit (RS) row, work in St st for ½"/1cm, end with a WS row.
ROW 1 (RS) K5, then rotate the LH needle counter-clockwise 360 degrees, then knit another 5 sts and rotate the LH needle again counter-clockwise 360 degrees. Cont to k5 and rotate LH needle, to the end of the row.
ROW 2 (WS) *P2tog; rep from * to end of row—25 sts.
ROW 3 (RS) K1, *k2tog; rep from * to end of row—13 sts.
ROW 4 (WS) P1, *p2tog; rep from * to end of row—7 sts. Cut yarn, leaving a long tail. Thread tail through rem sts. Draw up and secure. Sew center back seam. Sew flower to hat, using photo as a guide.✿

Lounging in Luxury

Take her to the spa in a robe and headband
of super-soft pure cashmere.

MATERIALS

- 3 0.88oz/25g skeins (each approx 82yd/75m) of Lion Brand Collection *Cashmere* (cashmere) in #106 cruise

- One pair size 6 (4mm) needles, OR SIZE TO OBTAIN GAUGE

- Stitch markers and holders

- Purchased emblem (optional)

GAUGE

22 sts and 30 rows to 4"/10cm over St st using size 6 (4mm) needles. *Take time to check gauge.*

K1, P1 RIB

(over an odd number of sts)
ROW 1 (RS) *K1, p1; rep from * to last st, k1.
ROW 2 P1, *k1, p1; rep from * to end.
Rep rows 1–2 for k1, p1 rib.

NOTE

Body is worked in one piece to armhole.

BODY

Cast on 111 sts. Work in k1, p1 rib for 3 rows, end with a RS row.
ROW 4 (RS) Sl 1, knit to end.
ROW 5 Sl 1, purl to end.
Rep last 2 rows until piece measures 4"/10cm from beg, end with a WS row.
NEXT (EYELET) ROW (RS) Sl 1, k3, yo, k2tog, *k4, yo, k2tog; rep from * to last 3 sts, k3.
NEXT ROW Sl 1, purl to end.
Work even until piece measures 4¾"/12cm from beg, end with a WS row.

NECK AND COLLAR SHAPING

ROW 1 (RS) Sl 1, p1, knit to last 2 sts, p2.
ROW 2 Sl 1, k1, purl to last 2 sts, k2.
ROW 3 Sl 1, p2, knit to last 3 sts, p3.
ROW 4 Sl 1, k2, purl to last 3 sts, k3.
ROW 5 Sl 1, p3, knit to last 4 sts, p4.
ROW 6 Sl 1, k3, purl to last 4 sts, k4.
ROW 7 Sl 1, p4, knit to last 5 sts, p5.
ROW 8 Sl 1, k4, purl to last 5 sts, k5.

DIVIDE FOR FRONTS AND BACK

NEXT ROW (RS) Sl 1, p5, k21, place these 27 sts on holder for right front, bind off next 6 sts for right armhole, k until there are 45 sts on needle, place these sts on holder for back, bind off next 6 sts for left armhole, k21, p6.

LEFT FRONT

ROW 1 Sl 1, k5, p21.
ROW 2 K20, p7.
ROW 3 Sl 1, k6, p20.
ROW 4 K19, p8.

ROW 5 Sl 1, k7, p19.
ROW 6 K18, p9.
ROW 7 Sl 1, k8, p18.
ROW 8 K17, p10.
ROW 9 Sl 1, k9, p17.
ROW 10 K16, p11.
ROW 11 Sl 1, k10, p16.
ROW 12 K15, p12.
ROW 13 Sl 1, k11, p15.
ROW 14 K14, p13.
ROW 15 Sl 1, k12, p14.
ROW 16 K13, p14.
ROW 17 Sl 1, k13, p13.
ROW 18 K12, p15.
ROW 19 Sl 1, k14, p12.
ROW 20 K11, p16.
ROW 21 Sl 1, k15, p11.
Place last 11 sts on holder for left shoulder—16 sts.

COLLAR EXTENSION
ROW 1 P16.
ROW 2 Sl 1, k15.
Rep last 2 rows until collar extension measures 2"/5cm, end with a WS row. Place sts on holder.

RIGHT FRONT
Place 27 sts from right front holder on needle, ready for a WS row.
ROW 1 (WS) Join yarn, p21, k6.
ROW 2 Sl 1, p6, k20.
ROW 3 P20, k7.
Cont as for left front, reversing all shaping.

BACK
Place 45 sts from back holder on needle, ready for a WS row.
ROW 1 (WS) Join yarn and p to end of row. Work a further 20 rows in St st, end with a WS row.
NEXT ROW (WS) P11, place these sts on holder for left shoulder, bind off center 23 sts, p11, place these sts on holder for right shoulder.

SLEEVES
Cast on 36 sts. Starting with a purl row, work 7 rows in St st.
NEXT (TURNING) ROW (WS) Purl.
Starting with a knit (RS) row, work in St st until piece measures 4"/10cm from turning row, end with a WS row. Bind off all sts.

FINISHING
With 3-needle bind-off, join 11 shoulder sts of back to front on each side. With 3-needle bind-off, join 16 sts of right and left collar extension. Sew collar extension to bound-off edge of back neck.

POCKETS (MAKE 2)
Cast on 19 sts. Starting with a purl (WS) row, work 15 rows in St st, end with a WS row. Work 2 rows in k1, p1 rib. Bind off in rib. Sew pockets to fronts, using photo as a guide.
Sew sleeve seams, working cuff seam on RS. Fold cuff to outside along turning row and tack in place. Set in sleeves.

TIE
Cast on 5 sts. Work in k1, p1 rib until piece measures 25"/63.5cm from beg. Bind off in rib. Thread tie in and out of eyelet row.

HEADBAND
Cast on 5 sts. Work in k1, p1 rib until piece measures 12"/30.5cm. Bind off in rib. Sew cast-on and bound-off edges together.

If desired, sew purchased emblem to left front of robe, using photo as a guide.✿

School Days

She'll be teacher's pet in this cheery sweater and skirt. Crisp white socks make it an A-plus ensemble!

MATERIALS

- 1 3¾oz/50g skein (each approx 100yd/91m) of Cascade Yarns *Fixation* (cotton/elastic) in #9054 calypso (A)
- 1 1½oz/100g skein (each approx 191yd/175m) of Cascade Yarns *Sierra* (cotton/wool) in #22 denim (B)
- 1 1¾oz/50g skein (each approx 170yd/155m) of Cascade Yarns *Heritage* (superwash merino/nylon) in #5682 white (C)
- One pair each sizes 6 and 7 (4 and 4.5mm) needles, OR SIZES TO OBTAIN GAUGE
- Spare size 6 (4mm) needle
- 1 set (4) size 2 (2.75mm) dpns, OR SIZE TO OBTAIN GAUGE
- Stitch markers and holders
- 2 small snaps
- 3 buttons (JHB Lady #99124 used in sample)
- Crochet hook and waste yarn
- Iron-on appliqué (optional)

GAUGES

20 sts and 28 rows to 4"/10cm over St st using size 7 (4.5mm) needles and A.
22 sts and 30 rows to 4"/10cm over St st using size 6 (4mm) needles and B.
28 sts and 36 rows to 4"/10cm over St st using size 2 (3mm) needles and C. *Take time to check gauges.*

K1, P1 RIB
(over an even number of sts)
ROW 1 (RS) *K1, p1; rep from * to end.
Rep row 1 for k1, p1 rib.

K1, P1 RIB
(over an odd number of sts)
ROW 1 (RS) K1, *p1, k1; rep from * to end.
ROW 2 *K1, p1; rep from * to last st, k1.
Rep rows 1 and 2 for k1, p1 rib.

PROVISIONAL CAST-ON
With crochet hook and waste yarn, crochet a chain several sts longer than the required number of sts to be cast on. Fasten off. With knitting needle, pick up and knit the required number of sts in the bumps of the chain, leaving a couple of empty chains at either end. When ready to return to the cast-on, "unzip" the sts by undoing the fastened-off end of the chain and pulling it out, placing the live sts on the knitting needle as you go.

NOTE
Work with yarn A relaxed; do not stretch.

SWEATER
BACK
With size 7 (4.5mm) needles and A, cast on 30 sts. Starting with a purl (WS) row, work in St st until piece measures 4"/10cm from beg, end with a WS row.

ARMHOLE SHAPING AND NECK OPENING
Bind off 2 sts at beg of next 2 rows—26 sts.
NEXT ROW (RS) Ssk, k11, cast on 1 st, join a second ball of yarn and cast on 1 st, k11, k2tog—13 sts each side. Working both sides at once, cont even in St st until armhole measures 2½"/6.5cm, end with a WS row. Place sts on holders for shoulders and back neck.

FRONT
With size 7 (4.5mm) needles and A, cast on 30 sts. Starting with a purl (WS) row, work in St st until piece measures 4"/10cm from beg, end with a WS row.

ARMHOLE SHAPING

Bind off 2 sts at beg of next 2 rows—26 sts.

NEXT ROW (RS) Ssk, knit to last 2 sts, k2tog—24 sts. Work even in St st until armhole measures 1½"/4cm, ending with a WS row.

NECK SHAPING

NEXT ROW (RS) K8, place center 8 sts on holder, join new yarn and k8. Work both sides at once, dec 1 st at each neck edge every RS row twice—6 sts rem each side for shoulder. Work even in St st until armhole measures same as back to shoulders. Place rem sts on holders.

SLEEVES

With size 7 (4.5mm) needles and A, cast on 22 sts. Work in k1, p1 rib for 3 rows, end with a RS row. Starting with a purl (WS) row, work 5 rows in St st, end with a WS row.

NEXT (INC) ROW (RS) K1, m1, knit to last st, m1, k1—24 sts. Cont in St st, rep inc row every 8th row twice more—28 sts. Work even until piece measures 4"/10cm from beg, ending with a WS row.

CAP SHAPING

Bind off 2 sts at beg of next 2 rows—24 sts.

NEXT ROW Ssk, knit to last 2 sts, k2tog—22 sts.
Purl 1 row. Bind off all sts loosely.

FINISHING

With 3-needle bind-off, join 6 shoulder sts of back to front on each side, leaving rem 7 sts each side of back on holder.

NECKBAND

With size 7 (4.5mm) needles, RS facing, and A, k7 from left back neck holder, pick up and k 8 sts down left front neck edge, k8 from front holder, pick up and k 8 sts up right front neck edge, k7 from right back holder—38 sts.
Work 6 rows in k1, p1 rib.
Bind off in rib.
Set in sleeves. Sew side and sleeve seams. Sew 2 small snaps to back opening, placing the first at neck edge and the remainder at middle of back opening. Apply appliqué to front of pullover, if desired, using photo as a guide.

SKIRT

With size 6 (4mm) needle and B, cast on 75 sts using provisional cast-on.

ROWS 1 AND 3 (WS) Purl.
ROW 2 Knit.
ROW 4 (TURNING RIDGE) (RS) Purl.
ROWS 5 AND 7 Purl.
ROW 6 Knit.
Carefully remove waste yarn, placing the 75 sts on spare needle. Hold spare needle behind working needle with WS tog.
ROW 8 (JOINING) (RS) *Insert a third needle into the first st on each needle and knit the two sts together; rep from * to end of row—75 sts.
ROW 9 Purl.
ROW 10 (RS) K18, pm, k39, pm, k18. Work 3 rows even in St st, end with a WS row.
ROW 14 (DEC) (RS) [Knit to 2 sts before marker, k2tog, sm, ssk] twice, knit to end of row—71 sts. Work 9 rows even.
Rep rows 14–23 once more, then row 14 once—63 sts. Work 3 rows even, end with a RS row.
Starting with row 2, work 3 rows in k1, p1 rib, end with a WS row. Bind off in rib.

FINISHING
BUTTONBAND

With size 6 (4mm) needles, RS facing, and B, pick up and k 29 sts along left front edge to turning ridge. Starting with row 2 of rib pat, work 4 rows in k1, p1 rib. Bind off in rib.

BUTTONHOLE BAND

With size 6 (4mm) needles, RS facing, and B, starting at turning ridge, pick up and k 29 sts along right front edge. Starting with row 2, work 1 row in k1, p1 rib.
NEXT ROW (RS) *[K1, p1] twice, k1, yo, k2tog; rep from * to last st, k1. Work 2 rows in rib, end with a RS row. Bind off in rib. Sew buttons to buttonband opposite buttonholes.

NEXT (DEC) RND K2tog, knit to last 2 sts, k2tog—34 sts. Work even in St st until piece measures 2¼"/5.5cm from beg.
NEXT (DEC) RND K2tog, knit to last 2 sts, k2tog—32 sts (11 sts on needles 1 and 3, 10 sts on needle 2). Work even in St st until piece measures 2½"/6.5cm from beg.
NEXT RND K11 from needle 1 to needle 3—22 heel sts. Leave 10 instep sts on hold.

HEEL
ROW 1 Sl 1, p21, turn.
ROW 2 (RS) Sl 1, knit to last 2 sts, turn.
ROW 3 Sl 1, purl to last 2 sts, turn.
ROW 4 Sl 1, knit to last 4 sts, turn.
ROW 5 Sl 1, purl to last 4 sts, turn.
ROW 6 Sl 1, knit to last 6 sts, turn.
ROW 7 Sl 1, purl to last 6 sts, turn.
ROW 8 Sl 1, knit to last 8 sts, turn.
ROW 9 Sl 1, purl to last 8 sts, turn. Slip 3 sts to right needle—11 sts each on needles 1 and 3.

FOOT
Resume working in the rnd.
NOTE To close gaps between heel and instep sts, *knit to gap, k1, pick up back loop of st below and place on left needle. Knit st and lifted st tog; rep from * for gap on opposite side.
RND 1 Knit.
RND 2 [K9, k2tog] (needle 1), k10 (needle 2), [k2tog, k9] (needle 3)—30 sts. Work even for 1½"/4cm.

FINISHING
Divide sts evenly on 2 needles as follows: sl first 7 sts on needle 1 to end of needle 3, sl last 3 sts on needle 1 to beg of needle 2, sl first 2 sts of needle 3 to end of needle 2—15 sts per needle. Turn to WS and join using 3-needle bind-off. ✿

SOCKS (MAKE 2)
CUFF
With C, cast on 36 sts and divide over 3 dpns as follows: 13 sts on needle 1, 10 sts on needle 2, and 13 sts on needle 3. Place marker for start of rnd and join, being careful not to twist. Work in St st (knit every rnd) until piece measures 1"/2.5cm from beg.

These socks match almost any outfit!
See page 75 for another look.

My Cozy Valentine

A traditional cabled dress and cap turn romantic with sparkling sequins and a beautiful berry hue.

MATERIALS

- 2 1¾oz/50g skeins (each approx 157yd/144m) of Lion Brand *Vanna's Sequins* (acrylic/polyester) in #146 merlot
- One pair size 3 (3.25mm) needles, OR SIZE TO OBTAIN GAUGE
- Cable needle (cn)
- Stitch markers and holders
- 4 small snaps

GAUGE

32 sts and 40 rows to 4"/10cm over stitch pat using size 3 (3.25mm) needles. *Take time to check gauge.*

K1, P1 RIB

(over an even number of sts)
ROW 1 (RS) *K1, p1; rep from * to end.
Rep row 1 for k1, p1 rib.

K2, P2 RIB

(over a multiple of 4 sts)
ROW 1 (RS) *K2, p2; rep from * to end.
Rep row 1 for k2, p2 rib.

CABLE PATTERN A

(over 4 sts)
ROWS 1 AND 3 (RS) K4.
ROWS 2 AND 4 P4.
ROW 5 4-st RC.
ROW 6 P4.
Rep rows 1–6 for cable pat A.

CABLE PATTERN B

(over 8 sts)
ROW 1 (RS) 4-st RC, 4-st LC.
ROW 2 AND ALL WS ROWS P8.
ROWS 3 AND 7 K8.
ROW 5 4-st LC, 4-st RC.
ROW 8 P8.
Rep rows 1–8 for cable pat B.

STITCH GLOSSARY

4-ST LC Sl 2 sts to cn and hold in *front*, k2, k2 from cn.
4-ST RC Sl 2 sts to cn and hold in *back*, k2, k2 from cn.

FRONT

Cast on 48 sts. Work in k1, p1 rib for 5 rows, end with a RS row.
SET-UP ROW (WS) K3, p4, k2, p8, k2, p4, k2, p4, k2, p8, k2, p4, k3.

BEG CABLE PATS
ROW 1 (RS) P3, [work row 1 of cable pat A over next 4 sts, p2, work row 1 of cable pat B over next 8 sts, p2, work row 1 of cable pat A over next 4 sts, p2] twice, p1.
ROW 2 K3, [work row 2 of cable pat A over next 4 sts, k2, work row 2 of cable pat B over next 8 sts, k2, work row 2 of cable pat A over next 4 sts, k2] twice, k1. Cont in pat as established, working appropriate row of each cable, until piece measures 7½"/19cm from beg, end with a WS row.

NECK SHAPING

NEXT ROW (RS) Work 19 sts in pat, place next 10 sts on holder for front neck, join a 2nd ball of yarn and work in pat to end of row. Working both sides at once, dec 1 st from each neck edge every RS row 5 times—14 sts rem each side for shoulder. Work even until piece measures 9"/23cm from beg, end with a WS row. Leave rem sts on holder.

BACK

Work as given for front until piece measures 6"/15cm from beg, end with a WS row.

BACK OPENING

NEXT ROW (RS) Pat 24 sts, join a 2nd ball of yarn and bind off center st, pat to end of row. Working both sides at once, work even until piece measures 9"/23cm from beg, end with a WS row. Leave rem sts on holder for shoulders and back neck.

SLEEVES

Cast on 34 sts. Work k1, p1 rib for 5 rows, end with a RS row.
SET-UP ROW (WS) K7, p4, k2, p8, k2, p4, k7.

BEG CABLE PATS

ROW 1 (RS) P7, work row 1 of cable pat A over next 4 sts, p2, work row 1 of cable pat B over next 8 sts, p2, work row 1 of cable pat A over next 4 sts, p7.
ROW 2 K7, work row 2 of cable pat A over next 4 sts, k2, work row 2 of cable pat B over next 8 sts, k2, work row 2 of cable pat A over next 4 sts, k7.
Cont as established, working appropriate row of cables. AT THE SAME TIME, inc 1 st at each end of 5th and every foll 6th row twice—40 sts. Work even in pat until piece measures 2¾"/7cm from beg, end with a WS row. Bind off all sts in pat.

FINISHING

With 3-needle bind-off, join 14 shoulder sts of back to front on each side, leaving rem 10 sts each side of back on holder.

NECKBAND

With RS facing and starting at left back neck, k 10 sts from holder, pick up and k 13 sts down left front, k 10 sts from front holder, pick up and k 13 sts up right front, k 10 sts from right back holder—56 sts. Work in k1, p1 rib for ¾"/2cm. Bind off in pat. Place markers 3"/7.5cm down from each shoulder on side edge of front and back for armholes. Set in sleeves between markers. Sew side and sleeve seams. Sew snaps to back opening, having the first ½"/1.5cm down from top of neck edge and the remainder spaced evenly along back opening.

HAT

Cast on 92 sts. Work in k2, p2 rib for 7 rows, end with a RS row.
ROWS 1, 3, AND 5 (WS) K2, *p4, k3; rep from * to last 6 sts, p4, k2.
ROWS 2 AND 4 P2, *k4, p3; rep from * to last 6 sts, k4, p2.
ROW 6 P2, m1p, *4-st RC, p3, m1p; rep from * to last 6 sts, 4-st RC, m1p, p2—106 sts.
ROWS 7, 9, AND 11 K3, *p4, k4; rep from * to last 7 sts, p4, k3.
ROWS 8 AND 10 P3, *k4, p4; rep from * to last 7 sts, k4, p3.
ROW 12 P3, m1p, *4-st RC, p4, m1p; rep from * to last 7 sts, 4-st RC, m1p, p3—120 sts.
ROWS 13, 15, 17, 19, 21, AND 23 K4, *p4, k5; rep from * to last 8 sts, p4, k4.

ROWS 14, 16, 20, AND 22 P4, *k4, p5; rep from * to last 8 sts, k4, p4.
ROW 18 P4, *4-st RC, p5; rep from * to last 8 sts, 4-st RC, p4.
ROW 24 P2, p2tog, *4-st RC, p3, p2tog; rep from * to last 8 sts, 4-st RC, p2tog, p2—106 sts.
ROWS 25, 27, AND 29 K3, *p4, k4; rep from * to last 7 sts, p4, k3.
ROWS 26 AND 28 P3, *k4, p4; rep from * to last 7 sts, k4, p3.
ROW 30 P1, p2tog, *4-st RC, p2, p2tog; rep from * to last 7 sts, 4-st RC, p2tog, p1—92 sts.
ROWS 31, 33, AND 35 K2, *p4, k3; rep from * to last 6 sts, p4, k2.
ROWS 32 AND 34 P2, *k4, p3; rep from * to last 6 sts, k4, p2.
ROW 36 P2tog, *4-st RC, p1, p2tog; rep from * to last 6 sts, 4-st RC, p2tog—78 sts.
ROW 37 K1, *p4, k2; rep from * to last 5 sts, p4, k1.
ROW 38 P1, *(k2tog) twice, p2tog; rep from * to last 5 sts, (k2tog) twice, p1—40 sts.
ROW 39 K1, *p2tog, k1; rep from * across—27 sts.
ROW 40 *K2tog; rep from * to last st, k1—14 sts.
ROW 41 *P2tog; rep from * to end—7 sts.
ROW 42 K2tog, k3, k2tog—5 sts. Draw yarn through rem sts, pull tight and secure. Sew center back seam. ✿

All Dolled Up

Which is sweeter: this lacy cardigan wrap or
the adorable vintage bunny who's admiring it?

MATERIALS

- 2 balls (each approx
160yd/147m) of Aunt Lydia's
Iced Bamboo 3 (viscose/metallic) in
#3585 lilac ice

- One pair size 4 (3.5mm) needles,
OR SIZE TO OBTAIN GAUGE

- Stitch markers

- 2 purchased ribbon roses

GAUGE

22 sts and 30 rows to 4"/10cm over
St st using size 4 (3.5mm) needles.
Take time to check gauge.

NOTES

1) Main body of wrap is worked
lengthwise in one piece.
2) Eyelet rib will naturally create a
bias fabric. Blocking will be
necessary to establish a
rectangular shape.
3) Pattern for the white socks
pictured can be found on page 69.

EYELET RIB PATTERN

(over multiple of 7 sts plus 3)
ROW 1 (WS) P3, *k4, p3; rep
from * to end.
ROW 2 K1, yo, k2tog, *p4,
k1, yo, k2tog; rep from * to end
of row.
Rep rows 1–2 for eyelet rib pat.

WRAP

LEFT FRONT
Cast on 52 sts. Starting with row
1, work in eyelet rib pat until
piece measures 5"/12.5cm from
beg, end with a RS row.

LEFT ARMHOLE SHAPING
NEXT ROW (WS) Work in pat
for 19 sts, bind off next 9 sts, work
in pat to end of row.
NEXT ROW Work in pat for 24
sts, cast on 9 sts over bound-off
sts, work in pat to end of row.

BACK
Cont even in pat for 5"/12.5cm,
end with a RS row.

RIGHT ARMHOLE
SHAPING
NEXT ROW (WS) Work in pat
for 19 sts, bind off next 9 sts, work
in pat to end of row.
NEXT ROW Work in pat for 24
sts, cast on 9 sts over bound-off
sts, work in pat to end of row.

RIGHT FRONT
Cont even in pat for 5"/12.5cm,
end with a RS row. Bind off.

SLEEVES
Cast on 30 sts.
ROW 1 P4, *k4, p3; rep from *,
end k5.
ROW 2 P5, *k1, yo, k2tog, p4;
rep from *, end k1, yo, k2tog, k1.
Rep last 2 rows three times more,
end with a RS row. Place markers
at each end of last row worked.
NEXT ROW (WS) Purl. Starting
with a knit (RS) row, work in St st
until piece measures 5"/12.5cm
from markers, end with a WS
row. Bind off.

FINISHING
Block main body of wrap to
establish a rectangular shape.
Sew sleeve seams, working cuff
seam from cast-on to markers on
RS. Fold cuff to outside and tack
if desired. Set in sleeves.
Sew ribbon roses to front edges
approx 3"/7.5cm from cast-
on/bound-off edge, using
photo as a guide. ✿

Vintage Bunny

MATERIALS

- 1 3½oz/100g skein (each approx 220yd/200m) Cascade Yarns *220 Superwash* (superwash wool) each in #817 aran (A) and #862 walnut heather (B)
- Small amounts pink and blue yarn
- Polyester fiberfill
- One set size 4 (3.5mm) needles, OR SIZE TO OBTAIN GAUGE
- One set (4) size 4 (3.5mm) dpn (double-pointed needles)
- Stitch marker

GAUGE

20 sts and 30 rows to 4"/10cm in St st using size 4 (3.5mm) needles. *Take time to check gauge.*

FRONT

With A, cast on 36 sts. Work in St st for 10 rows. Bind off 12 sts at beg of next two rows for hind legs.

Continue working in St st on remaining 12 sts for 32 rows more.

NEXT ROW Cast on 12 sts each at beg and end of row for front legs—36 sts. Continue in St st for 8 rows more.

Bind off 12 sts at beg of next two rows—12 sts.

DEC ROW 1 [K2tog] 6 times—6 sts.

Purl one row.

DEC ROW 2 [K2tog] 3 times—3 sts.

Bind off rem sts.

BACK

With B, cast on 12 sts.

Work in garter st (knit every row) for 18 rows.

Cast on 20 sts at beg and end of following row, cont working in garter st for 10 rows more.

Bind off 12 sts at beg of following two rows for hind legs—28 sts.

Cont working in garter st for 6 rows more.

NEXT (INC) ROW (RS) K1, M1, knit to last st, M1, k1.

Rep inc row every other row 7 times more—44 sts.

Knit one row.

NEXT (DEC) ROW K1, k2tog, knit to last 3 sts, SKP, k1.

Rep dec row 11 times more—20 sts.

Work even in garter st for 6 rows.

Cast on 10 sts at beg and end of following row for front legs.

Work even in garter st for 10 rows.

Bind off 12 sts at beg of following 2 rows—16 sts.

Divide remaining sts evenly among 3 dpns and join to work in the round. Place marker for beg of round, work even in garter st for 10 rnds.

NEXT (DEC) RND K1, k2tog, k to last 3 sts, SKP, k1.

Rep dec rnd 6 times more—4 sts. Thread yarn through rem sts and pull tight.

EARS

With B, cast on 8 sts.

ROW 1 *K to last st, sl last st purlwise. Rep from * for 2" from cast-on.

ROW 2 (DEC) K1, k2tog, k to last 3 sts, SKP, sl last st purlwise.

Repeat rows 1 & 2 twice more—4 sts.

Rep row 1 once more.

SK2P, bind off.

FINISHING

Sew front to back, leaving bottom flap open for stuffing. Stuff and sew flap shut. Sew ears in place, folding in half at bottom to create shape.

Embroider eyes and nose with blue and pink yarn, using photo as guide.

With A, cut 8 lengths of yarn, 4" each, for whiskers, and run through nose as shown.

With A, make ½" pompom for tail, or use a purchased pompom.✿

Picnic in the Park

Get ready for summertime fun with a bright and cheery sundress, purse, and flower-adorned headband.

MATERIALS

- 1 2.8oz/80g 8-pack of skeins (each approx 38yd/35m) of Lion Brand *Bonbons* (cotton) in #640 nature
- One pair size 3 (3.25mm) needles, OR SIZE TO OBTAIN GAUGE
- Size D-3 (3.25mm) crochet hook
- Stitch holders
- 3 small snaps
- 4 buttons, ½"/1cm diameter (JHB #103711 DD-48 used in sample)
- 1 small gold bead

GAUGE

30 sts and 36 rows to 4"/10cm over pat st using size 3 (3.25mm) needles. *Take time to check gauge.*

CHEVRON PATTERN

(over multiple of 10 sts plus 3)
ROW 1 (RS) K1, ssk, *k7, S2KP; rep from * to last 10 sts, k7, k2tog, k1.
ROW 2 P5, *[p1, yo, p1] into next st, p7; rep from * to last 6 sts, [p1, yo, p1] into next st, p5.
Rep rows 1–2 for chevron pat.

STRIPE PATTERN

[2 rows white (B), 2 rows green (C), 2 rows pink (D), 2 rows tan (E), 2 rows brown (F), 2 rows light orchid (G), 2 rows green (C), 4 rows yellow (H), 2 rows purple (A)] twice, 2 rows white (B), 2 rows green (C), 2 rows pink (D), 2 rows tan (E), 2 rows brown (F), 2 rows light orchid (G), 2 rows green (C), 4 rows yellow (H).

NOTE

Body is made in one piece.

DRESS

Starting at lower edge, with A, cast on 103 sts. Knit 1 (WS) row. Starting with row 1, work in chevron pat, following stripe pat to end. Cont in A as follows:

BODICE SHAPING

ROW 1 (RS) K1, *k2, k2tog; rep from * to last 2 sts, k2—78 sts.
ROW 2 (WS) Inc 1 into first st, *k1, p1; rep from * to last sts, k1—79 sts.
Cont in k1, p1 rib for 6 rows more. Break A and join G.
ROW 9 (RS) Knit.
ROW 10 Work in k1, p1 rib as established.
ROW 11 (RS) Bind off 26 sts in rib, work next 7 sts in rib and place on holder for left shoulder strap, bind off next 13 sts, work next 7 sts in rib and place on holder for right shoulder strap, bind off rem 26 sts in rib.

SHOULDER STRAPS

Place 7 sts from right shoulder strap holder on needle, ready for a WS row.
ROW 1 (WS) Join yarn, work in k1, p1 rib as established. Cont in rib for 4.5"/11.5cm. Bind off in rib. Rep for left shoulder strap.

FINISHING

Sew center back seam, leaving a 2"/5cm opening at the top. Sew bound-off edge of straps to back. Sew 2 snaps along center back opening, placing the first at top edge and the second 1"/2.5cm below. Sew 2 buttons over snaps. Sew 2 buttons to front bodice, using photo as a guide.

HEADBAND

With D, cast on 7 sts. Work in k1, p1 rib for 12"/30.5cm. Bind off in rib. Sew snap to headband at cast-on and bound-off edge.

FLOWER

With H, cast on 63 sts. Knit 1 row. Starting with row 1, work 2 rows in chevron pat with D, 2 rows with G, end with a WS row.

ROW 6 (RS) With C, *K2tog; rep from * to last st, k1—32 sts.

ROW 7 With C, *k2tog; rep from * to end of row—16 sts.

ROW 8 With B, *P2tog; rep from * to end of row—8 sts. Cut yarn, leaving a long tail. Thread tail through rem sts. Draw up and

secure. Sew seam. Sew flower to headband, using photo as a guide.

BAG

With F, cast on 19 sts. Work in garter st for 4"/10cm. Break F and join E.

ROW 1 (RS) With E, work in garter st for ½"/1cm, end with a RS row.

DEC ROW (RS) Ssk, knit to last 2 sts, k2tog—17 sts. Knit next row.
Rep last 2 rows once more—15 sts.

ROW 5 (RS) Bind off all sts knitwise, decreasing 1 st at each end of row. Fasten off.
Fold F section in ½"/1cm (E section becomes flap). With crochet hook and E, starting at lower fold edge on one side, work sc to join bag side edges, ch 60 for handle, work sc to join remaining side edges. Fasten off. Sew bead to front flap, using photo as a guide. ✿

Monkeying Around

The monkeys at the zoo aren't as colorful as this!
A matching hat and scarf are playful as can be.

MATERIALS
- 1 2.8oz/80g 8-pack of skeins (each approx 38yd/35m) of Lion Brand *Bonbons* (acrylic) in #620 pastels
- One pair size 3 (3.25mm) needles, OR SIZE TO OBTAIN GAUGE
- Size D-3 (3.25mm) crochet hook
- One set (2) size 3 (3.25mm) dpn
- 2 easy-sew eyes, 8mm diameter
- Polyester fiberfill

GAUGE
24 sts and 32 rows to 4"/10cm over St st using size 3 (3.25mm) needles. *Take time to check gauge.*

K1, P1 RIB
(over an even number of sts)
ROW 1 (RS) *K1, p1; rep from * to end.
Rep row 1 for k1, p1 rib.

NOTES
1) Use colors as follows for hat: green (A), yellow (B), medium blue (C), pink (D), peach (E), white (F).
2) Use colors as follows for scarf: green (A), white (B), pink (C), medium blue (D), purple (E), light blue (F), peach (G).
3) Each flap on scarf is worked separately, then all flaps are joined on the same row.
4) Break yarn on all but last flap on scarf and leave sts on needle.

HAT
With A, cast on 56 sts. Work in St st until piece measures 1¼"/3cm from beg, end with a WS row. Break A and join B. Work in St st until piece measures 2¾"/7cm from beg, end with a WS row. Break B and join C. Work 4 rows in St st. Break C and join D. Work 4 rows in St st. Break D and join A.

TOP SHAPING
ROW 1 (RS) K2tog, *SK2P, k7; rep from * to last 4 sts, SK2P, k1—43 sts. Purl one row.

ROW 3 (RS) K1, *SK2P, k5; rep from * to last 2 sts, k2—33 sts. Purl one row .
ROW 5 (RS) K1, *SK2P, k3; rep from * to last 2 sts, k2tog—22 sts. Break A and join E.
ROW 6 (WS) Purl.
ROW 7 (RS) K1, *SK2P, k1; rep from * to last st, k1—12 sts.
ROW 8 *P2tog; rep from * to end of row—6 sts. Draw yarn though rem sts, pull tight and secure. Sew center back seam.

FINISHING
MOUTH
With F, cast on 3 sts.
ROW 1 (RS) Knit.
ROW 2 Purl.
ROW 3 Kfb, k1, kfb—5 sts. Starting with a purl (WS) row, work in St st for 4"/10cm, end with a WS row.
ROW 1 (DEC) (RS) K2tog, k1, k2tog—3 sts. Work 1 row even.
ROW 3 (DEC) (RS) SK2P—1 st. Fasten off. With E and stem stitch, embroider center of mouth, using photo as a guide.

EARS (MAKE 2)

With D, cast on 8 sts, leaving a long tail for seaming.

ROW 1 (RS) *Kfb across—16 sts. Starting with a purl (WS) row, work 9 rows in St st, end with a WS row.

ROW 11 *K2tog; rep from * to end—8 sts. Draw yarn though rem sts, pull tight and secure. Fold in half to shape.

EAR FLAPS (MAKE 2)

With A, cast on 11 sts. Starting with a knit (RS) row, work in St st for 1¼"/3cm, end with a WS row.

ROW 1 (DEC) (RS) K1, ssk, k5, k2tog, k1—9 sts.

ROW 2 AND ALL WS ROWS Purl.

ROW 3 (RS) K1, ssk, k3, k2tog, k1—7 sts.

ROW 5 (RS) K1, ssk, k1, k2tog, k1—5 sts.

Change to dpns.

ROW 7 (I-CORD) *K3, slide sts to opposite end of needle, do not turn. Rep from * until I-cord measures 3"/7.5cm.

NEXT ROW K3tog. Fasten off.

BALL TOP

With C, cast on 8 sts, leaving a long tail for seaming.

ROW 1 (RS) *Kfb across—16 sts. Starting with a purl (WS) row, work 9 rows in St st, end with a WS row.

ROW 11 *K2tog; rep from * to end—8 sts. Draw yarn through rem sts, pull tight and secure. Stuff with fiberfill. Sew center back seam.

Mark center front of hat. Sew on mouth, ears, and eyes, using photo as a guide.

NOSE

With C, make 2 French knots as nostrils between eyes and mouth, using photo as a guide. Sew RS of ear flaps to WS of hat at sides, along last row of A. Sew ball top to hat.

SCARF

1ST FLAP

With A, cast on 8 sts. Work in k1, p1 rib for 1¼"/3cm. Break yarn, leaving sts on needle.

2ND AND 9TH FLAP

With B, on same needle, cast on 8 sts. Work in k1, p1 rib for 1"/2.5cm. Break yarn, leaving sts on needle.

3RD AND 11TH FLAP

With C, on same needle, cast on 8 sts. Work in k1, p1 rib for 1½"/4cm. Break yarn, leaving sts on needle.

4TH FLAP

With D, work as given for 2nd flap.

5TH FLAP

With E, work as given for 1st flap.

6TH AND 13TH FLAP

With F, work as given for 3rd flap.

7TH FLAP

With G, work as given for 2nd flap.

8TH FLAP

With A, work as given for 3rd flap.

10TH FLAP

With C, work as given for 1st flap.

12TH FLAP

With E, work as given for 2nd flap.

14TH FLAP

With G, work as given for 1st flap.

15TH FLAP

With A, work as given for 3rd flap. Do not break yarn.

ROW 1 (JOINING ROW) (WS) With A, work in k1, p1 rib across all flaps—120 sts. Work a further 4 rows in k1, p1 rib, end with a WS row. Break A and join B.

ROW 6 (RS) With B, *k8, p8; rep from * to last 8 sts, k8.

ROW 7 P8, *k8, p8; rep from * to end of row.

Rep last 2 rows once more, then first row once. Break B and join A.

ROW 11 (WS) With B, work in k1, p1 rib to end of row. Work a further 2 rows in rib. Bind off all sts in rib.

TIE

With crochet hook and C, make a chain approx 18"/45.5cm in length. Fasten off. Thread tie through center of k8, p8 rib, using photo as a guide. Knot each end of tie. ✿

Heads Up!

These three whimsical, brightly colored toppers will enliven any outfit.

MATERIALS

- 1 2.8oz/80g 8-pack of skeins (each approx 38yd/35m) of Lion Brand *Bonbons* (acrylic) in #620 pastels

- One pair each sizes 2, 3, and 4 (2.75, 3.25, and 3.5mm) needles, OR SIZES TO OBTAIN GAUGE

- One set (2) size 3 (3.25mm) dpn (double-pointed needles), for bee

- Stitch holders

- Small amount of polyester fiberfill, for bee

- Small amount of black yarn for bee eyes

- 2 easy-sew eyes, 8mm diameter, for owl

GAUGE

24 sts and 32 rows to 4"/10cm over St st using size 4 (3.5mm) needles. *Take time to check gauge.*

K2, P2 RIB

(over multiple of 4 sts)
ROW 1 (RS) *K2, p2; rep from * to end.
Rep row 1 for k2, p2 rib.

NOTE

One 8-pack of skeins makes all three hats.

BEEHIVE HAT

NOTE Use colors as follows: medium blue (A), peach (B), light blue (C), white (D), green (E), pink (F), yellow (G).
With size 4 (3.5mm) needles and A, cast on 56 sts.
ROWS 1–9 Starting with a purl (WS) row, work in St st, end with a WS row.
ROWS 10–16 With B, knit. Change to size 3 (3.25mm) needles.
ROWS 17–22 With A and starting with a purl (WS) row, work in St st, end with a WS row.
ROWS 23–28 With B, purl.
ROWS 29–33 With A and starting with a purl (WS) row, work in St st, end with a WS row.
ROWS 34–39 With B, knit.
ROWS 40–41 With A and starting with a knit (RS) row, work in St st, end with a WS row.

TOP SHAPING

ROW 42 (RS) With A, *k2tog; rep from * to end of row—28 sts.
ROWS 43 AND 45 With A, purl.
ROW 44 With A, *k2tog; rep from * to end of row—14 sts.
ROW 46 With A, *k2tog; rep from * to end of row—7 sts.
Draw yarn through rem sts, pull tight and secure. Sew center back seam.

BEE BODY

With size 2 (2.75mm) needles and C, cast on 8 sts, leaving a long tail for sewing.
ROW 1 Kfb in each st—16 sts.
ROW 2 AND ALL WS ROWS Purl.
ROWS 3, 5, 7, AND 9 Knit.
ROWS 11 AND 12 *K2tog; rep from * to end of row—4 sts.
ROW 13 Pass 1st, 2nd, and 3rd sts over 4th st—1 st. Fasten off. Stuff body with a small amount of polyester fiberfill. Sew side edges together.

HEAD

With size 2 (2.75mm) needles and C, cast on 1 st.
ROW 1 Kfb—2 sts.
ROW 2 AND ALL WS ROWS Purl.
ROW 3 Kfb in each st—4 sts.
ROW 5 Knit.
ROW 7 [K2tog] twice—2 sts. Pass rem st over first—1 st. Fasten off. Stuff head with a small amount of polyester fiberfill. Sew side edges together. Sew head to body.

WINGS (MAKE 2)

With size 3 (3.25mm) dpns and D, cast on 3 sts.
ROW 1 K3, slide sts to opposite end of needle, do not turn. Rep

last row until piece measures 2"/5cm. Bind off. Sew wings to body at body/head seam. With black yarn, embroider 2 small eyes, using photo as a guide.

FLOWER

With size 3 (3.25mm) needles and F, cast on 35 sts.

ROW 1 (WS) *K1, bind off 5 sts (2 sts on RH needle); rep from * to end—10 sts. Draw yarn though rem sts, pull tight and secure. With G, make a French knot in center of flower.

LEAF

With size 3 (3.25mm) needles and E, cast on 5 sts.

ROW 1 (RS) K2, yo, k1, yo, k2—7 sts.
ROW 2 AND ALL EVEN ROWS Purl.
ROW 3 K3, yo, k1, yo, k3—9 sts.
ROW 5 K4, yo, k1, yo, k4—11 sts.
ROW 7 Ssk, k7, k2tog—9 sts.
ROW 9 Ssk, k5, k2tog—7 sts.
ROW 11 Ssk, k3, k2tog—5 sts.
ROW 13 Ssk, k1, k2tog—3 sts.
ROW 15 SK2P—1 st.
Fasten off.

FINISHING

Sew bee, flower, and leaf to top of hat, using photo as a guide.✿

Mix and match these hats with the scarf on page 81!

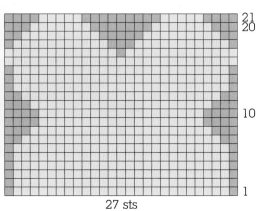

27 sts

KITTY HAT

NOTE Use colors as follows: purple (A), pink (B), light blue (C), white (D), medium blue (E). With size 3 needles and A, cast on 56 sts. Work 4 rows in k2, p2 rib, increasing 1 st at center of last row—57 sts.

BEG CHART PAT

ROW 1 (RS) With A, k15, work row 1 of chart over next 27 sts; with A, k15.

ROW 2 With A, p15, work row 2 of chart over next 27 sts; with A, p15.

Cont as established, working appropriate row of chart to end, end with a RS row.

Cont in A only.

ROW 22 (WS) Purl.

TOP SHAPING

ROW 23 (RS) *K2tog; rep from * to last st, k1—29 sts. Work 1 row even.

ROW 25 (RS) *K2tog; rep from * to last st, k1—15 sts. Work 1 row even.

ROW 27 (RS) *K2tog; rep from * to last st, k1—8 sts.

Draw yarn though rem sts, pull tight and secure. Sew center back seam.

FINISHING

EARS (MAKE 2)

With D, cast on 9 sts. Work 6 rows in garter st.

ROW 7 (RS) *Ssk, knit to last 2 sts, k2tog—7 sts.

ROW 8 Knit.

Rep last 2 rows twice more—3 sts.

ROW 13 (RS) Sl 1, k2tog, psso—1 st. Fasten off.
Sew ears in place.

EMBROIDERY

EYES: With E and running stitch, embroider eyes, using photo as a guide.

MOUTH: With C and running stitch, embroider mouth, using photo as a guide.

WHISKERS: With D, embroider 3 whiskers on each side of nose, using photo as a guide.✿

OWL HAT

NOTE Use colors as follows: yellow (A), light blue (B), peach (C). Hat is worked in one piece and seamed at center back. With size 3 needles and A, cast on 58 sts. Work 11 rows in garter st, end with a WS row.

Starting with a knit (RS) row, work in St st until piece measures 3"/7.5cm from beg, end with a WS row. Break A and join B. Work a further 6 rows in St st, end with a WS row.

ROW 7 (RS) Bind off 10 sts, k10 and place these 10 sts on holder for first ear, bind off next 18 sts, k10 and place these 10 sts on holder for second ear, bind off rem 10 sts.

FIRST EAR

Place 10 sts from first ear holder on needle, ready for a WS row. Starting with a purl (WS) row, cont in St st, dec 1 st at each end of every RS row 4 times—2 sts. Bind off.

SECOND EAR

Place 10 sts from second ear holder on needle, ready for a WS row.

Starting with a purl (WS) row, cont in St st, dec 1 st at each end of every RS row 4 times—2 sts. Bind off.

FINISHING

Sew center back seam. Fold hat in half, matching center front to center back seam. Sew top of hat and ear seam.

EYES (MAKE 2)

With B, loosely cast on 25 sts. Knit 3 rows. Draw yarn through sts, pull tight, leaving a ½"/1.5cm opening at center, and secure. Using photo as guide, sew eyes to front of hat. Sew easy-sew eyes to hat, inside eye opening.

BEAK

With C, embroider a diamond shape between eyes, using a long stitch. ✿

Alice's Tea Party

Soft shades of gray and blue meet soft ruffles
for an effect that's pure cream and sugar.

MATERIALS
- 1 1¾ oz/50g skein (each approx 425yd/390m) of Debbie Bliss *Rialto Lace* (merino) each in #4003 light gray (A) and #4018 turquoise (B)
- One pair size 2 (3mm) needles, OR SIZE TO OBTAIN GAUGE
- Size D-3 (3.25mm) crochet hook
- Stitch holder
- 2 small snaps
- 10 seed beads

GAUGE
30 sts and 38 rows to 4"/10cm over St st using size 2 (3mm) needles. *Take time to check gauge.*

3-NEEDLE JOIN
With RS of ruffles facing and the needles parallel, insert a third needle into the first st on each needle and knit the two stitches together.

STRIPE PATTERN
Working in St st throughout, [2 rows B, 2 rows A] 10 times, 2 rows B, 6 rows A.
Rep for stripe pat.

NOTES
1) Sleeves are worked from the top down to wrist.
2) Dress is worked in one piece to bodice.

DRESS
RUFFLES
(MAKE 2, 1 USING B AND 1 USING A)
Cast on 72 sts. Knit 1 (WS) row. Starting with a knit (RS) row, work in St st for 1"/2.5cm, end with a WS row.
ROW 9 (RS) *K2tog; rep from * to end—36 sts.
ROW 10 Purl. Place sts on spare needle.

SKIRT
With A, cast on 126 sts. Starting with a knit (RS) row, work in St st for 8 rows.

BEG STRIPE PAT
Work the 48 rows of stripe pat, end with a WS row.
ROW 57 (RS) With A, k9, *k2tog; rep from * to last 9 sts, k9—72 sts. Work 1 row even.

DIVIDE FOR FRONT AND BACK BODICE
ROW 59 (RS) K18 and place these 18 sts on holder for left back, k36 and place these sts on holder for front, k18 for right back.

RIGHT BACK BODICE
Working on the 18 sts for right back, work even in St st until piece measures 4½"/11.5cm from dividing row, end with a WS row. Bind off all sts.

LEFT BACK BODICE
Place 18 sts from left back holder on needle, ready for a WS row. With A, work even in St st until piece measures 4½"/11.5cm from dividing row, end with a WS row. Bind off all sts.

FRONT BODICE
Place 36 sts from front holder on needle, ready for a WS row. With A and starting with a purl (WS) row, work 7 rows in St st, end with a WS row.
ROW 8 (JOINING ROW) (RS) With RS facing and A, hold sts of ruffle (worked in B) in front of front bodice sts and, using 3-needle join, knit across—36 sts. Work a further 9 rows in St st, end with a WS row.

ROW 18 (JOINING ROW)
(RS) With RS facing and A, hold sts of ruffle (worked in A) in front of front bodice sts and, using 3-needle join, knit across—36 sts. Work a further 9 rows in St st, end with a WS row.

ROW 28 (JOINING ROW)
(RS) With RS facing and A, hold sts of ruffle (worked in B) in front of front bodice sts and, using 3-needle join, knit across—36 sts. Work a further 7 rows in St st, end with a WS row.

NECK SHAPING
ROW 36 (RS) K12, join a 2nd ball of yarn, and bind off center 12 sts, k12. Working both sides at once, bind off 2 sts from each neck edge once—10 sts rem each side. Work even in St st until piece measures 4½"/11.5cm from dividing row, end with a WS row. Bind off rem sts each side for shoulder.

SLEEVES
With B, cast on 34 sts. Starting with a knit (RS) row, work in St st, dec 1 st each end of 5th and every following 6th row 4 times—24 sts. Work even until piece measures 4"/10cm from beg, end with a WS row. Bind off.

FINISHING
Sew shoulder seams. Place markers 2"/5cm down from each shoulder on side edge of front and back for armholes. Set in sleeves between markers. Sew side and sleeve seams.

NECK RUFFLE
With A, cast on 120 sts. Knit 1 (WS) row. Starting with a knit (RS) row, work in St st for 8 rows, end with a WS row.
ROW 10 (RS) *K2tog; rep from * to end—60 sts.
ROW 11 Purl. Bind off all sts. Place neck ruffle in front on neck opening. With crochet hook, RS facing, and A, working through both ruffle and neck edging, work 1 row sc evenly around neck opening. Fasten off. With

crochet hook, RS facing and A, work 1 row of sc evenly along back opening. Sew 2 small snaps to back opening, placing the first at neck edge and the second at middle of back opening.

HEADBAND
With A, cast on 72 sts. Work 24 rows following stripe pat, end with a WS row. Bind off. Fold cast-on edge to WS, making ¼"/0.5cm hem. Rep for bound-off edge. Sew ends tog, gather seam and secure.

FLOWER
With A, cast on 72 sts. Work in St st for 8 rows. Break A and join B.
ROW 9 (RS) *K3tog; rep from * to end—24 sts.
ROW 10 *P3tog; rep from * to end—8 sts. Draw yarn through rem sts, pull tight and secure. Sew seed beads to center of flower. Sew flower to gathered area on headband.✿

Coat of Many Colors

Glittering stripes on a coat, hat, and legwarmers make for a head-turning outerwear set—with a purse to match!

MATERIALS

- 1 2.8oz/80g 8-pack of skeins (each approx 38yd/35m) of Lion Brand *Bonbons* (acrylic/metallic polyester) in #650 party
- One pair size 3 (3.25mm) needles, OR SIZE TO OBTAIN GAUGE
- Size D-3 (3.25mm) crochet hook
- Cable needle
- 3 snaps
- 5 buttons (4 for coat, 1 for bag) (JHB Kali #71220 used in sample)

GAUGE

24 sts and 36 rows to 4"/10cm over St st using size 3 (3.25mm) needles. *Take time to check gauge.*

K2, P2 RIB

(multiple of 4 sts)

ROW 1 (RS) *K2, p2; rep from * to end.

Rep row 1 for k2, p2 rib.

K2, P2 RIB

(multiple of 4 sts plus 2)

ROW 1 (RS) *K2, p2; rep from * to last 2 sts, k2.

ROW 2 P2, *k2, p2; rep from * to end.

Rep rows 1 and 2 for k2, p2 rib.

BODY STRIPE PATTERN

ROWS 1–6 With B, work in St st.

ROW 7 With C, *k1, sl 1 wyif; rep from * to end.

ROWS 8–12 With C, work in St st.

ROW 13 With D, *k1, sl 1 wyif; rep from * to end.

ROWS 14–16 With D, work in St st.

ROWS 17–32 Rep rows 1–16, changing colors to E, F, and G.

ROWS 33–48 Rep rows 1–16, changing colors to H, A, and C.

ROWS 49–64 Rep rows 1–16, changing colors to D, G, and F.

ROWS 65–72 Rep rows 1–8, changing colors to E and C.

NOTES

1) Body is worked in one piece to armhole.

2) Colors are as follows: copper (A), light copper (B), gold (C), purple (D), magenta (E), royal (F), wheat (G), red (H). One 8-skein pack makes all three projects.

COAT

With A, cast on 78 sts. Work in k2, p2 rib for 4 rows. Starting with row 1, work in body stripe pat through row 46, end with a WS row.

DIVIDE FOR FRONTS AND BACK

ROW 47 (RS) Work in pat for 16 sts, place these 16 sts on holder for right front, bind off next 4 sts for right armhole, work in pat until there are 38 sts on needle, place these sts on holder for back, bind off next 4 sts for left armhole, work in pat for last 16 sts.

LEFT FRONT

Working on last 16 sts only, work even in pat through row 67, end with a RS row.

NECK SHAPING

NEXT ROW (WS) Bind off 5 sts, work in pat to end of row. Cont in pat, dec 1 st at neck edge every RS row once more—10 sts. Work even to end of body stripe pat, end with a WS row. Bind off rem sts.

RIGHT FRONT

Place 16 sts from right front holder onto needle, ready for a WS row. Work even in pat through row 68, end with a WS row.

NECK SHAPING

ROW 69 (RS) Bind off 5 sts, pat to end of row. Cont in pat, dec 1 st at neck edge every RS row once more—10 sts. Work even to end of body stripe pat, end with a WS row. Bind off rem sts.

BACK

Place 38 sts from back holder on needle, ready for a WS row. Work even in pat through row 67 has been worked, end with a RS row.

BACK PLEAT

ROW 68 (WS) P15, sl next center 8 sts to cable needle and hold to front (do *not* work these sts), p15.

ROW 69 (RS) K11, knit next 8 sts together with sts on cable needle (8 sts dec), k11—30 sts. Cont even to end of body stripe pat, end with a WS row. Bind off rem sts.

SLEEVES

With B, cast on 22 sts. Work in k2, p2 rib for 4 rows, end with a WS row. Break B and join D.

ROW 1 With D, *k1, sl 1 wyif; rep from * to end. Starting with a purl (WS) row, work in St st, increasing 1 st at each end of 4th and every following 4th row 4 times more—32 sts. Work even in St st until piece measures 3"/7.5cm from beg, end with a WS row. Break D and join E.

BEGIN PATTERN

ROW 1 (RS) With E, *k1, sl 1 wyif; rep from * to end.

ROW 2 With E, purl.

ROW 3 *With E, k2; with G, k3; rep from * to last 2 sts, with E, k2.

ROW 4 With E, p2, *with G, p3; with E, p2; rep from * to end of row. With E, work 2 rows in St st. Break E and join F.

ROW 7 (RS) With F, *k1, sl 1 wyif; rep from * to end. Work 3 rows in St st, end with a WS row. Break F and join C.

ROW 11 (RS) With C, *k1, sl 1 wyif; rep from * to end. Work 5 rows in St st, end with a WS row. Break C and join H.

ROW 17 (RS) With H, *k1, sl 1 wyif; rep from * to end. Work 5 rows in St st, end with a WS row. Bind off.

FINISHING

Sew shoulder seams. Sew sleeve seams. Set in sleeves.

LEFT FRONT BAND

With RS facing and C, pick up and k 56 sts evenly along left front edge. Work in k2, p2 rib for 7 rows, ending with a WS row. Break C and join A.

ROW 8 (RS) With A, knit.

ROW 9 (WS) Work in k2, p2 rib as established. Bind off in rib.

RIGHT FRONT BAND

Work as given for left front band.

COLLAR

With RS facing and A, pick up and k 50 sts evenly around neck opening, starting and ending at front band pickup row. Work in k2, p2 rib for 2¾"/7cm, end with a WS row. Bind off in rib. Sew buttons to right front band, placing the first button ½"/1.5cm down from neck edge, the last ½"/1.5cm up from cast-on edge, and the remaining 2 buttons spaced evenly between. Sew one half of snap to WS of right front band under top 2 buttons and the remaining half to RS of left front band to correspond.

HAT

With F, cast on 66 sts. Work in k2, p2 rib for 4 rows, end with a WS row.

ROW 1 (RS) With G, *k1, sl 1 wyif; rep from * to end.

ROWS 2–6 With G, work in St st.

ROWS 7–12 Rep rows 1–6 using H.

ROWS 13–18 Rep rows 1–6 using B.

ROWS 19–24 Rep rows 1–6 using D.

ROWS 25–28 Rep rows 1–4 using E.

TOP SHAPING

ROW 29 With E, k1, *k2tog, k2; rep from * to last st, k1—50 sts.

ROW 30 With E, purl.

ROW 31 With A, *k1, sl 1 wyif; rep from * to end.

ROWS 32, 34, AND 36 With A, purl.

ROW 33 With A, k1, [k2tog] 24 times, k1—26 sts.

ROW 35 With A, k1, [k2tog] 12 times, k1—14 sts.

ROW 37 With A, [k2tog] 7 times—7 sts. Draw yarn through rem sts, pull tight and secure. Sew center back seam.

CORKSCREWS (MAKE 5 USING G, H, A, F, AND E)

Loosely cast on 15 sts.

ROW 1 (RS) Knit in front, back, and front of each st—45 sts. Bind off. Twist into shape. Sew to top of hat, using photo as a guide.

BAG

With G, cast on 23 sts. Knit 2 rows. Cont in St st until piece measures 5"/12.5cm from beg, end with a WS row. Break G and join H.

FLAP

ROW 1 With H, *k1, sl 1 wyif; rep from * to last st, k1.

ROWS 2–4 With H, work in St st. Break H and join F.

ROW 5 With F, *k1, sl 1 wyif; rep from * to end.

ROWS 6–9 With H, work in St st.

ROW 10 (WS) With H, knit. Bind off knitwise.

FINISHING

Fold up cast-on edge 2"/5cm. Sew side seams. Fold colorwork portion down for flap. Sew button at center of flap, using photo as a guide. Sew one half of snap to WS of flap under button and the remaining half to RS of bag to correspond.

STRAP

With crochet hook and H, ch 65. Fasten off. Sew ends of chain to side edges of bag.

LEGWARMERS (MAKE 2)

With E, cast on 34 sts. Work in k2, p2 rib for 4 rows, end with a WS row. Break E and join F.

ROWS 1–10 With F, work in St st. Break F and join H.

ROW 11 With H, *k1, sl 1 wyif; rep from * to end.

ROWS 12–16 With H, work in St st. Break H and join A.

ROW 17 With A, *k1, sl 1 wyif; rep from * to end.

ROWS 18–22 With A, work in St st. Break A and join H.

ROW 23 With H, knit. Starting with a WS row, work in k2, p2 rib for 4 rows, end with a RS row. Bind off in rib. Sew center back seam.✿

Feeling Groovy

Step back in time and stay cool with this '60s-inspired fur-trimmed coat and hat, with funky matching socks.

MATERIALS

- 1 2.8oz/79g skein (each approx 45yd/41m) of Prism Yarns *Plume* (nylon) in periwinkle (A)
- 1 1¾oz/50g skein (each approx 175yd/160m) of Koigu *KPPPM* (merino) in #101 (B)
- 1 1¾oz/50g skein (each approx 175yd/160m) of Koigu *KPPPM* (merino) in #410 (C)
- One pair size 10 (6mm) needles, OR SIZE TO OBTAIN GAUGE
- 1 set (4) size 2 (2.75mm) dpns, OR SIZE TO OBTAIN GAUGE
- Stitch markers
- 3 snaps

GAUGES

12 sts and 16 rows to 4"/10cm over St st using size 10 (6mm) needles with 2 strands B held together.

28 sts and 36 rows to 4"/10cm over St st using size 2 (2.75mm) needles and C. *Take time to check gauges.*

NOTE

Coat is knit sideways from right center front to left center front using 2 strands of B held together throughout.

COAT
RIGHT FRONT

With 2 strands B held tog, cast on 30 sts. Work in garter st (knit every row) for 4 rows. Change to A and cont in garter st until piece measures 2"/5cm from beg, placing marker at end of last WS row. Change to 2 strands B, starting with a knit (RS) row, work in St st for 1¼"/3cm, ending with a WS row.

ARMHOLE SHAPING
ROW 1 (RS) Bind off 10 sts, knit to end of row—20 sts.

BACK
ROW 2 P20, cast on 10 sts—30 sts.
Cont in St st for 1¼"/3cm, placing marker at end of last WS row. Change to A, cont in St st for 3"/7.5cm. Change to 2 strands B, starting with a knit (RS) row, work in St st for 1¼"/3cm, ending with a WS row.

ARMHOLE SHAPING
ROW 1 (RS) Bind off 10 sts, knit to end of row—20 sts.

LEFT FRONT
ROW 2 P20, cast on 10 sts—30 sts.
Cont in St st for 1¼"/3cm, placing marker at end of last WS row. Change to A and work in garter st for 1½"/4cm. Change to 2 strands B, knit 4 rows. Bind off all sts knitwise.

SLEEVE
With A, cast on 14 sts. Knit 2 rows. Change to 2 strands B.

Starting with a knit (RS) row, work in St st, inc 1 st at each end of 5th and every following 4th row twice—20 sts. Work even until piece measures 4½"/11.5cm from beg, end with a WS row. Bind off all sts.

FINISHING

Sew shoulder seams, matching front and back markers. Sew sleeve seams. Set in sleeves. Sew 3 snaps evenly down coat front, having the first snap at neck edge and the last 2"/5cm from lower edge and the remaining snap spaced evenly between.

HAT

With A, cast on 40 sts. Knit 1 (WS) row. Change to 2 strands B and starting with a knit (RS) row, work in St st for 8 rows, end with a WS row.

CROWN SHAPING

ROW 10 (RS) *SK2P, k5; rep from * to end of row—30 sts. Work 1 row even.

ROW 12 *SK2P, k3; rep from * to end of row—20 sts. Work 1 row even.

ROW 14 *SK2P, k1; rep from * to end of row—10 sts. Work 1 row even.

ROW 16 *K2tog; rep from * to end of row—5 sts. Draw yarn through rem sts, pull tight and secure. Sew center back seam.

SOCKS (MAKE 2)
CUFF

With C, cast on 36 sts and divide over 3 dpns as follows: 13 sts on needle 1, 10 sts on needle 2, and 13 sts on needle 3. Place marker for start of rnd and join, being careful not to twist sts. Work in St st (knit every rnd) until piece measures 1"/2.5cm from beg.

DEC RND 1 K2tog, knit to last 2 sts, k2tog—34 sts.
Work even in St st until piece measures 2¼"/5.5cm from beg.

DEC RND 2 K2tog, knit to last 2 sts, k2tog—32 sts (11 sts on needles 1 and 3, 10 sts on needle 2). Work even in St st until piece measures 2½"/6.5cm from beg.

ROW 1 K11 from needle 1 to needle 3—22 heel sts. Leave 10 instep sts on hold.

HEEL

ROW 2 Sl 1, p21, turn.
ROW 3 (RS) Sl 1, knit to last 2 sts, turn.
ROW 4 Sl 1, purl to last 2 sts, turn.

ROW 5 Sl 1, knit to last 4 sts, turn.
ROW 6 Sl 1, purl to last 4 sts, turn.
ROW 7 Sl 1, knit to last 6 sts, turn.
ROW 8 Sl 1, purl to last 6 sts, turn.
ROW 9 Sl 1, knit to last 8 sts, turn.
ROW 10 Sl 1, purl to last 8 sts, turn. Slip 3 sts to right needle—11 sts on each of needles 1 and 3.

FOOT

Resume working in the rnd.

NOTE To close gaps between heel and instep sts, *knit to gap, k1, pick up back loop of st below and place on left needle. Knit st and lifted st tog; rep from * for gap on opposite side.
RND 1 Knit.
RND 2 [K9, k2tog] (needle 1), k10 (needle 2), [k2tog, k9] (needle 3)—30 sts. Work even for 1½"/4cm.

FINISHING

Divide sts evenly on 2 needles as follows: sl first 7 sts on needle 1 to end of needle 3, sl last 3 sts on needle 1 to beg of needle 2, sl first 2 sts of needle 3 to end of needle 2—15 sts per needle. Turn to WS and join using 3-needle bind-off. ✿

Tiny Dancer

Pair this rose-embellished capelet, purse, and cap with tulle and tights: perfect for a prima ballerina!

MATERIALS
- 1 1¾oz/50g skein (each approx 83yd/76m) of Lucci Yarns *Pom Pom* (nylon) in lavender (A)
- 1 1¾ oz/50g skein (each approx 98yd/90m) of Sirdar *Funky Fur Magic* (polyester) in #602 (B)
- One pair size 10 (6mm) needles, OR SIZE TO OBTAIN GAUGE
- Stitch markers
- 1yd/1m ribbon, ¼"/64mm wide
- 7 small satin roses
- 1 small crown stick pin (if desired)

GAUGE
12 sts and 16 rows to 4"/10cm over rev St st using size 10 (6mm) needles and one strand each of A and B held together.
Take time to check gauge.

NOTE
The pattern used to make the cape (two pieces) is used to make both hat and bag (each one piece).

CAPE
RIGHT HALF
With one strand each of A and B held together, cast on 31 sts. Starting with a knit (WS) row, work in rev St st until piece measures 1"/2.5cm. Place marker at each end of next row and work even until piece measures 2½"/6.5cm from beg, end with a RS row.

ROW 1 (DEC)(WS) K1, [k2tog] 15 times; rep from * to end—16 sts.
ROW 2 (DEC) *P2tog; rep from * to end—8 sts.
ROW 3 (DEC) *K2tog; rep from * to end—4 sts. Pass 1st, 2nd, and 3rd sts over 4th st—1 st. Fasten off.

LEFT HALF
Work as given for right half. Sew right and left halves together along one side edge from cast-on edge to marker (center back seam). Leave rem side edge open for front opening.

TIES
Cut two 6"/15cm lengths of ribbon. Secure ribbon to each half along front opening at marker. Sew ribbon rose to left front, using photo as a guide. Attach crown stick pin to left front, if desired.

HAT
With one strand each of A and B held together, cast on 31 sts. Starting with a knit (WS) row, work in rev St st until piece measures 2½"/6.5cm from beg, end with a RS row.

ROW 1 (DEC)(WS) K1, [k2tog] 15 times; rep from * to end—16 sts.
ROW 2 (DEC) *P2tog; rep from * to end—8 sts.
ROW 3 (DEC) *K2tog; rep from * to end—4 sts. Pass 1st, 2nd, and 3rd sts over 4th st—1 st. Fasten off. Sew center back seam. Sew 3 ribbon roses to hat, using photo as a guide.

HANDBAG
Work as given for hat. Sew center back seam.

HANDLES
Cut two 6"/15cm lengths of ribbon. Sew ribbon to cast-on edge to form a loop, using photo as a guide. Sew 3 ribbon roses to hat, using photo as a guide. ✿

Stripes Ahoy

Ready to set sail? A nautical-themed dress, sunhat, and purse are perfect for a day at the shore.

MATERIALS
- 1 1¾ oz/50g skein (each approx 180yd/165m) of Grignasco *Champagne* (merino/silk) each in #800 ecru (A), #1122 blue (B), and #1116 yellow (C)
- One pair size 3 (3.25mm) needles, OR SIZE TO OBTAIN GAUGE
- Stitch holders and markers
- 4 small snaps
- 1 iron-on appliqué with nautical theme (optional)
- 1 button, ¾"/2cm diameter (JHB #20222 used in sample)

GAUGE
26 sts and 36 rows to 4"/10cm over St st using size 3 (3.25mm) needles. *Take time to check gauge.*

K1, P1 RIB
(over an odd number of sts)
ROW 1 (RS) *K1, p1; rep from * to last st, k1.
ROW 2 P1, *k1, p1; rep from * to end.
Rep rows 1–2 for k1, p1 rib.

K2, P2 RIB
(over multiple of 4 sts)
ROW 1 (RS) *K2, p2; rep from * to end.
Rep row 1 for k2, p2 rib.

STRIPE PATTERN
In St st, work *2 rows A, 2 rows B; rep from * for stripe pat.

NOTES
1) Skirt is knit in one piece vertically and gathered horizontally for waist.
2) Bodice is knit in one piece to armhole.

DRESS
SKIRT
With B, cast on 30 sts. Starting with a knit row, work in St st for 4 rows. Cont even, following stripe pat, until piece measures approx 18½"/47cm, ending with 2 rows B. Work a further 2 rows in B. Bind off.

BODICE
With RS facing and B, starting and ending 2 rows from cast-on/bound-off edge, pick up and k 150 sts evenly along one long edge of skirt.
NEXT ROW (WS) P3, *p3tog; rep from * to last 3 sts, p3—54 sts. Work 14 rows following stripe pat, end with 2 rows A and a WS row.

DIVIDE FOR FRONT AND BACKS
NEXT ROW (RS) With B, k12, place these 12 sts on holder for left back, bind off next st for left armhole, knit until there are 28 sts on needle, place these sts on holder for front, bind off next st for right armhole, knit last 12 sts for right back.

RIGHT BACK
Keeping continuity of stripe pat, work a further 23 rows, end with a WS row. Bind off all sts.

LEFT BACK
Place 12 sts from left back holder on needle, ready for a WS row. Keeping continuity of stripe pat, work a further 23 rows, end with a WS row. Bind off all sts.

FRONT
Place 28 sts from front holder on needle, ready for a WS row. Keeping continuity of stripe pat, work a further 15 rows, end with a WS row.

NECK SHAPING
NEXT ROW (RS) K10, join a 2nd ball of yarn and bind off center 8 sts, k10. Working both sides at once, dec 1 st at each neck edge every RS row twice— 8 sts rem each side. Work even in

stripe pat until armhole measures same as back. Bind off rem 8 sts each side, for shoulders.

SLEEVES

With C, cast on 74 sts. Knit 3 rows, placing markers at each end of last row. Break C and join B. Starting with 2 rows B, cont in stripe pat, dec 1 st at each end of 3rd and every RS row 6 times more—60 sts.

NEXT ROW (RS) With B, *k2tog; rep from * to end of row—30 sts. Work 1 row even. Bind off. Weave a length of yarn through bound-off edge and pull tightly to gather.

FINISHING

Sew shoulder seams. Sew sleeve seam from cast-on edge to marker. Set in sleeves, adjusting gathers as required.

RIGHT BACK BAND

With RS facing and B, starting at neck edge, pick up and k 36 sts evenly along right center back edge to start of bodice. Work in k2, p2 rib for 5 rows. Bind off in rib.

LEFT BACK BAND

With RS facing and B, starting at bodice, pick up and k 36 sts evenly along left center back edge to neck edge. Work in k2, p2 rib for 5 rows. Bind off in rib.

NECKBAND

With RS facing and C, pick up and k 48 sts evenly around neck edge, including back bands. Knit 3 rows. Bind off all sts knitwise.

SKIRT HEM EDGING

With RS facing and C, pick up and k 140 sts evenly around lower edge of skirt. Knit 3 rows. Bind off all sts knitwise. Sew skirt center back seam.

Place right back band over left back band and sew through both thicknesses to skirt.

Mark position for 3 snaps on back opening of top, placing the first at neck edge, the last ½"/1.5cm from start of bodice, and the remainder spaced evenly between. Sew one half of snap to WS of right back at markers and the remaining half to RS of left back. If desired, sew applique in place at center front, using photo as a guide.

HAT

With C, cast on 112 sts. Knit 4 rows, end with a WS row. Starting with a knit (RS) row, work in St st until piece measures 1½"/4cm from beg, end with a WS row.

NEXT (DEC) ROW (RS) K1, *k2tog; rep from * to last st, k1—57 sts. Starting with row 2, work in k1, p1 rib for 3 rows, end with a WS row. Starting with a knit (RS) row, work even in St st for 14 rows, end with a WS row.

SHAPE TOP

ROW 1 *K5, k2tog; rep from * to last st, k1—49 sts.

ROW 2 AND ALL WS ROWS Purl.

ROW 3 *K4, k2tog; rep from * to last st, k1—41 sts.

ROW 5 *K3, k2tog; rep from * to last st, k1—33 sts.

ROW 7 *K2, k2tog; rep from * to last st, k1—25 sts.

ROW 9 *K1, k2tog; rep from * to last st, k1—17 sts.

ROW 11 *K2tog; rep from * to last st, k1—9 sts. Cut yarn, leaving a long tail. Thread tail through rem sts. Draw up and secure. Sew center back seam.

BAG

With A, cast on 21 sts. Knit 8 rows, end with a WS row. Break A and join B. Starting with a knit row, work in St st until piece measures 1½"/4cm from beg, placing markers at each end of St st until piece measures 4½"/11.5cm from markers, end with a RS row. Knit 3 rows. Bind off all sts knitwise.

Fold bag in half, matching bound-off edge to markers. Sew side seams. Sew half of snap to WS of flap and remaining half to RS of bag. Sew decorative button over snap on RS of flap, using photo as a guide.

With crochet hook and 2 strands of B held together, join with a slip stitch to side seam. Ch 60. Fasten off. Attach chain to remaining side seam. ✿

Winter Wonderland

The ultimate in cold-weather luxe: a fur-trimmed
Nordic outfit straight from the lodge in Aspen.

MATERIALS
- 1 1¾oz/50g skein (each approx 180yd/165m) of Grignasco *Champagne* (wool/silk) each in #726 ice blue (A) and #800 ecru (B)
- One pair size 3 (3.25mm) needles, OR SIZE TO OBTAIN GAUGE
- Stitch markers and holders
- 1yd/1m fur trim
- 6 ½"/1.5cm buttons in light blue (JHB Rosalind #42196 used in sample)
- 6 snaps

GAUGE
30 sts and 34 rows to 4"/10cm over Fair Isle pat using size 3 (3.25mm) needles.
Take time to check gauge.

K1, P1 RIB
(over an odd number of sts)
ROW 1 (RS) *K1, p1; rep from * to last st, k1.
ROW 2 P1, *k1, p1; rep from * to end.
Rep rows 1 and 2 for k1, p1 rib.

NOTE
Jacket body is worked in one piece to armhole.

JACKET
With B, cast on 93 sts.
ROW 1 (RS) Work 5 sts in k1, p1 rib, knit to last 5 sts, work last 5 sts in k1, p1 rib. Rep last row 3 times more, end with a WS row.

BEG CHART 1
ROW 1 (RS) With B, work 5 sts in rib, work row 1 of chart 1 to rep line, work 5-st rep 15 times, work to end of chart; with B, work 5 sts in rib.
Cont as established, keeping first and last 5 sts in rib until end of row 7 (RS).
ROW 8 (WS) With B, work 5 sts in rib, work row 8 of chart 1 over next 83 sts, increasing 2 sts evenly across; with B, work 5 sts in rib—95 sts.

BEG CHART 2
ROW 1 (RS) With B, work 5 sts in rib, starting where indicated for body, work row 1 of chart to rep line, work 6-st rep 13 times, work to end of chart where indicated for body; with B, work 5 sts in rib.
Cont as established, keeping first and last 5 sts in rib until end of row 24 (piece measures approx 4"/10cm from beg), end with a WS row.

DIVIDE FOR FRONTS AND BACK
ROW 25 (RS) Keeping continuity of chart, work in pat for 23 sts, place these 23 sts on holder for right front, bind off next 6 sts for right armhole, work in pat until there are 37 sts on needle, place these sts on holder for back, bind off next 6 sts for left armhole, work last 23 sts in pat.

LEFT FRONT
Cont even in pat through chart row 40.
ROW 41 (RS) With A, bind off 10 sts for shoulder, place rem 13 sts on holder.

RIGHT FRONT
Place 23 sts from right front holder on needle, ready for a WS row. Cont even in pat to chart row 40.
ROW 41 (RS) With B, rib 5 sts, k8, place these 13 sts on holder, bind off rem 10 sts for shoulder.

BACK
Place 37 sts from right back holder on needle, ready for a WS row. Starting with a WS row, cont even in pat through chart row 40.

ROW 41 (RS) With A, bind off 10 sts, k until there are 17 sts on needle, bind off rem 10 sts. Place rem 17 sts on holder.

SLEEVES
With B, cast on 30 sts. Work in k1, p1 rib for 2"/5cm, end with a WS row. Starting with a knit (RS) row, work in St st, inc 1 st at each end of 3rd and every following 4th row 4 times—40 sts. Work even until piece measures 6"/15cm from beg, end with a WS row.

CAP SHAPING
Bind off 3 sts at beg of next 2 rows. Dec 1 st at each end of next and every RS row once more, end with a WS row—30 sts. Bind off.

Sew shoulder seams. Place sts from fronts and back holders onto needle, ready for a RS row—43 sts.

HOOD
ROW 1 (RS) With B, work 5 sts in rib, M1, [k1, M1] twice, [k2, M1] 14 times, [k1, M1] twice, k1, rib 5 sts—62 sts.
ROW 2 (WS) With B, rib 5 sts, purl to last 5 sts, rib 5 sts.
ROW 3 With B, rib 5 sts, knit to last 5 sts, rib 5 sts.
ROW 4 With B, rib 5 sts, purl to last 5 sts, rib 5 sts.

BEG CHART 3
With B, work 5 sts in rib. Work row 1 of chart 3 to next rep line, work 3-st rep 15 times, work to end of chart; with B, rib 5 sts. Cont as established, keeping first and last 5 sts in rib until end of row 8 of chart.

BEG CHART 2
ROW 1 (RS) With B, work 5 sts in rib. Starting where indicated for hood, work row 1 of chart 2 to rep line, work 6-st rep 7 times, work to end of chart where indicated for hood; with B, work 5 sts in rib.
Cont as now established, keeping first and last 5 sts in rib until end of row 28. With B, work 2 rows in St st. Bind off all sts. Fold top of hood in half with WS together and sew. Sew fur to hood front and around bottom edge of jacket.
Sew sleeve seams, reversing seam for cuff turn-back. Set in sleeves. Sew 3 buttons along right front edge, placing the first button at start of neck shaping, the last 1¼"/3cm from cast-on

edge, and the remaining button spaced evenly between. Sew one half of snap to WS behind buttons, and sew the remaining half to RS of opposite end of band to correspond.

COWL
With B, cast on 72 sts.
ROW 1 (RS) Work 5 sts in k1, p1 rib, knit to last 5 sts, work last 5 sts in k1, p1 rib. Rep last row 3 times more, end with a WS row.

BEG CHART 4
ROW 1 (RS) With B, work 5 sts in rib, work row 1 of chart 4 to rep line, work 30-st rep twice, work to end of chart 4; with B, work 5 sts in rib.
Cont as est, keeping first and last 5 sts in rib until end of row 16 of chart, end with a WS row.
ROW 17 (RS) With B, work 5 sts in k1, p1 rib, knit to last 5 sts, work last 5 sts in k1, p1 rib. Rep last row 3 times more, end with a WS row. Bind off all sts knitwise. Sew 3 buttons, using photo as a guide, placing the first button ½"/1.5cm from bound-off edge, the last ½"/1.5cm from cast-on edge, and the remainder spaced evenly between. Sew on snaps as for jacket.

CHART 1

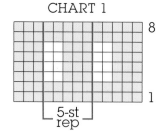

8

1

5-st
rep

CHART 3

8

1

3-st
rep

CHART 2

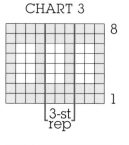

40

30

20

10

1

6-st
rep

end
body

start
body

end
hood

start
hood

PANTS

LEGS (MAKE 2)
Beg at waist with A, cast on 35 sts. Work in k1, p1, rib for 4 rows, end with a WS row. Starting with a knit (RS) row, work in St st until piece measures 3½"/9cm from beg, end with a WS row.

CROTCH SHAPING
Cast on 3 sts at beg of next 2 rows—41 sts. Work 4 rows even.

LEG SHAPING
Dec 1 st at beg and end of next and every following 6th row 5 times more—29 sts.
Work even until piece measures 10"/25.5cm from beg, end with a RS row. Knit 3 rows. Bind off all sts knitwise.

FINISHING
Sew leg seams. Sew center front and back seam. ✿

COLOR KEY
▨ ice blue (A)
☐ ecru (B)

CHART 4

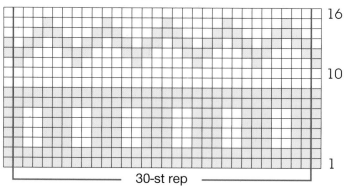

16

10

1

30-st rep

Fetching in Flowers

The floral embellishments and pretty edgings on this jacket and cap are classic "Nicky"!

MATERIALS
- 2 1¾oz/50g skeins (each approx 191yd/175m) of Red Heart *Stardust* (wool/nylon) in #1530 purple
- 1 skein DMC *Coton Perlé 3* (cotton) each in #963, #3805, and #907
- One pair size 2 (2.75mm) needles, OR SIZE TO OBTAIN GAUGE
- Spare size 2 (2.75mm) needle (for 3-needle join)
- One size C-2 crochet hook
- Stitch markers and holders

GAUGE
30 sts and 40 rows to 4"/10cm over pat st using size 2 (2.75mm) needles. *Take time to check gauge.*

K1, P1 RIB
(over an even number of sts)
ROW 1 (RS) *K1, p1; rep from * to end.
Rep row 1 for k1, p1 rib.

SEED STITCH
(over an even number of sts)
ROW 1 (WS) *K1, p1; rep from * to end.
ROW 2 *P1, k1; rep from * to end.
Rep rows 1 and 2 for seed st.

SEED STITCH
(over an odd number of sts)
ROW 1 (RS) K1, *p1, k1; rep from * to end.
Rep row 1 for seed st.

3-NEEDLE JOIN
With RS of layers facing and the needles parallel, insert a third needle into the first st on each needle and work the two sts together.

NOTE
Body of jacket is worked in one piece to armhole.

JACKET
UPPER LAYER
Cast on 108 sts. Work in seed st for 6 rows, end with a WS row.
ROW 7 (RS) Work 6 sts in seed st, rotate LH needle counter-clockwise 360 degrees, then work in pat for another 6 sts and rotate LH needle again counter-clockwise 360 degrees. Cont to work in pat for 6 sts and rotate LH needle to the end of the row. Break yarn and place sts on spare needle.

MAIN BODY
Cast on 116 sts.
ROW 1 (WS) P4, work in seed st to last 4 sts, p4.
ROW 2 K4, work in seed st to last 4 sts, k4.
Rep last 2 rows twice more, end with a RS row.
ROW 7 (WS) P4, work 6 sts in seed st, rotate LH needle counter-clockwise 360 degrees, then work in pat for another 6 sts and rotate LH needle again counter-clockwise 360 degrees. Cont to work in pat for 6 sts and rotate LH needle to the last 4 sts, p4.
Work even in pat for 8 rows, end with a WS row.
ROW 16 (JOINING ROW) (RS) K4, with RS facing, hold sts of upper layer in front of body sts; working in pat, use 3-needle join over next 108 sts, k4 —116 sts. Work even in pat for 13 rows.

ROW 30 (DEC) (RS) K4, [(p1, k1) 4 times, p2tog] 10 times, (p1, k1) 4 times, k4—106 sts.

ROW 31 P4, *k1, p1; rep from * to last 4 sts, p4.

ROW 32 K4, *k1, p1; rep from * to last 4 sts, k4.

Rep last 2 rows once more, end with a RS row.

ROW 35 (WS) P4, work in seed st to last 4 sts, p4.

ROW 36 K4, work in seed st to last 4 sts, k4.

Work even in pat until piece measures 4"/10cm above top of ribbing, ending with a WS row.

DIVIDE FOR FRONTS AND BACK

ROW 1 (RS) Work in pat for 23 sts, place last 23 sts on holder for right front, bind off next 8 sts for right armhole, work in pat until there are 44 sts on needle, place these sts on holder for back, bind off next 8 sts for left armhole, pat rem 23 sts for left front.

LEFT FRONT

ROW 2 (WS) Work in pat to end of row.

ROW 3 K2tog, work in pat to end of row.

NECK SHAPING

ROW 4 (WS) Bind off 4 sts, work in pat to end of row—18 sts. Cont in pat, dec 1 st at armhole edge every RS row twice more—16 sts. Work even until armhole measures 2¾"/7cm, end with a RS row.

ROW 1 (WS) Bind off 9 sts in pat, work in pat to end of row—7 sts.

COLLAR EXTENSION

Cont even in pat on rem 7 sts until extension measures 1½"/4cm from shoulder bind-off, end with a WS row. Bind off in pat.

RIGHT FRONT

Place 23 sts from right front holder on needle, ready for a WS row. Work 1 row even in pat.

NECK SHAPING

ROW 2 (RS) Bind off 4 sts, work in pat to last 2 sts, k2tog—18 sts. Cont in pat, dec 1 st at armhole edge every RS row twice more—16 sts. Work even until armhole measures 2¾"/7cm, end with a WS row.

ROW 1 (RS) Bind off 9 sts in pat, work in pat to end of row—7 sts.

COLLAR EXTENSION

Cont even in pat on rem 7 sts until extension measures 1½"/4cm from shoulder bind-off, end with a WS row. Bind off in pat.

BACK

Place 44 sts from back holder on needle, ready for a WS row. Keeping continuity of pat, work in pat, dec 1 st at each end of every RS row 3 times—38 sts.

Work even in pat until armhole measures 2¾"/7cm, end with a WS row. Bind off in pat.

SLEEVES
UPPER LAYER

Cast on 30 sts. Work in seed st for 6 rows, end with a WS row.

ROW 7 (RS) Work 6 sts in seed st, rotate the LH needle counter-clockwise 360 degrees, then work in pat for another 6 sts and rotate the LH needle again counter-clockwise 360 degrees. Cont to work 6 sts in pat and rotate LH needle to end of row. Break yarn and place sts on spare needle.

MAIN SLEEVE

Cast on 30 sts. Work in seed st for 6 rows, end with a WS row.

ROW 7 (RS) Work 6 sts in seed st, rotate the LH needle counter-clockwise 360 degrees, then work in pat for another 6 sts and rotate the LH needle again counter-clockwise 360 degrees. Cont to work in pat for 6 sts and rotate LH needle to end of row.

ROW 16 (JOINING ROW) (RS) With RS facing, hold sts of upper layer in front of main sleeve sts and, working in pat, use 3-needle join across row—30 sts.

Cont in pat, inc 1 st at each end of 2nd and every following 4th row 6 times more—44 sts. Work even in pat until piece measures 2½"/6.5cm from joining row, end with a WS row.

CAP SHAPING

Bind off 4 sts at beg of next 2 rows—36 sts. Dec 1 st at each end of next and every following RS row twice more, end with a WS row—30 sts. Bind off loosely in pat.

FINISHING

Sew shoulder seams. Sew sleeve seams. Set in sleeves. Sew bound-off edges of collar extension together. Sew collar extension to back neck edge.

COLLAR

Cast on 50 sts. Work in seed st for 6 rows, end with a WS row.
ROW 7 (RS) K1, work 6 sts in seed st, rotate LH needle counterclockwise 360 degrees, then work in pat for another 6 sts and rotate LH needle again counterclockwise 360 degrees. Cont to work in pat for 6 sts and rotate LH needle to last st, k1.
Work 3 rows even in seed st. Bind off in pat.
Sew WS of collar to RS of neck extension, starting and ending at neck shaping.

JACKET TIE

With crochet hook, make a chain 25"/63.5cm in length. Fasten off. Thread tie in and out through sts of k1, p1 rib, using photo as a guide.

EMBROIDERY

Using daisy stitch for the petals, a French knot for the center, and straight stitch for the leaves, embroider flowers on jacket, using photo as a guide.

HAT
UPPER LAYER

Cast on 92 sts.
ROW 1 (WS) P1, work pat row 1 to last st, p1.
ROW 2 K1, work pat row to last st, k1.
ROWS 3–6 Rep rows 1 and 2 twice.
ROW 7 (WS) P1, work 6 sts in seed st, rotate LH needle counterclockwise 360 degrees, then work in pat for another 6 sts and rotate LH needle again counterclockwise 360 degrees. Cont to work in pat for 6 sts and rotate LH needle to last st, p1. Break yarn and place sts on spare needle.

LOWER LAYER

Cast on 92 sts.
ROW 1 (WS) P1, work pat row 1 to last st, p1.
ROW 2 K1, work pat row to last st, k1.
ROWS 3–6 Rep rows 1 and 2 twice.
ROW 7 (WS) P1, work 6 sts in seed st, rotate LH needle counterclockwise 360 degrees, then work in pat for another 6 sts and rotate LH needle again counterclockwise 360 degrees. Cont to work in pat for 6 sts and rotate LH needle to last st, p1.

Work even in pat for 8 rows, end with a WS row.
ROW 16 (JOINING ROW) (RS) With RS facing, hold sts of upper layer in front of lower layer sts and, working in pat as established, use 3-needle join across row—92 sts.
Work even in pat until piece measures 3"/7.5cm from joining row, end with a WS row.

CROWN SHAPING

ROW 1 (RS) K1, *k2tog; rep from * to last st, k1—47 sts.
ROWS 2, 4, AND 6 Knit.
ROW 3 K1, *k2tog; rep from * to end of row—24 sts.
ROW 5 K1, *k2tog; rep from * to last st, k1—13 sts.
ROW 7 K1, *k2tog; rep from * to end of row—7 sts.
ROW 8 P1, (p2tog, p1) twice—5 sts.
Draw yarn through rem sts, pull tight and secure. Sew center back seam.

FINISHING

Using daisy stitch for the petals, a French knot for the center, and straight stitch for the leaves, embroider flowers on hat, using photo as a guide. ✿

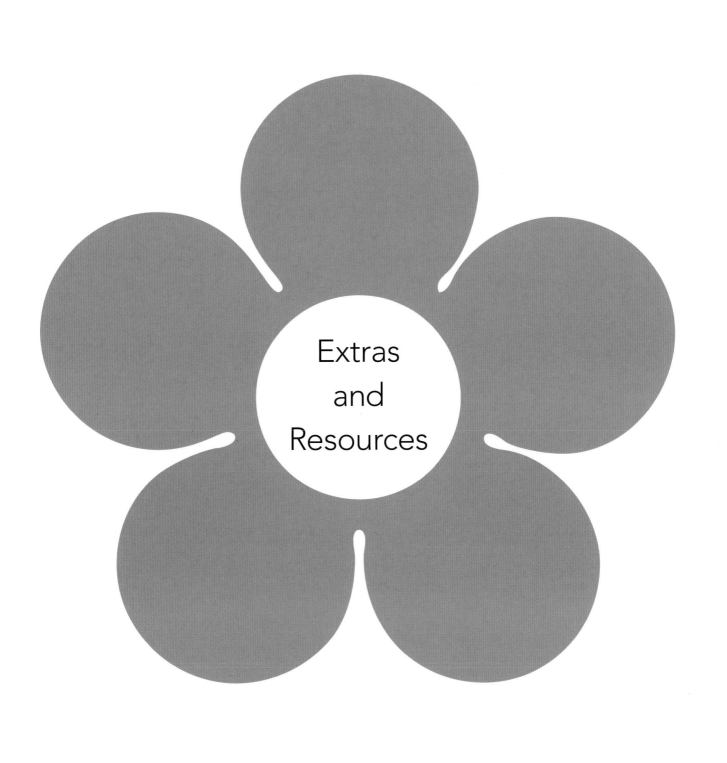

Extras
and
Resources

A Little Bit of Bling

It's fun and easy to make jewelry that matches your doll's outfits!

SKULLDUGGERY BRACELET

Wineglass markers make great bracelets.
See page 51.

WHAT A HOOT! CHOKER

A purchased beaded bracelet makes a lovely necklace.
See page 58.

SCHOOL DAYS BEADED BRACELET

A big-girl bracelet can work if you wrap it around the doll's wrist twice.
See page 64.

PICNIC IN THE PARK NECKLACE

String small beads or pearls on elastic thread, making sure the elastic is long enough to stretch over the doll's head.
See page 78.

PERFECT MATCH TENNIS BRACELET

Ribbons or yarn can be used as tie closures, or clasps can be purchased and attached to broken chains, etc. Beads can be restrung.
See page 27.

MY COZY VALENTINE PENDANT

Purchase a chain bracelet and add a charm.
See page 70.

Sweets for the Sweet

Bake some tasty treats as sweet as your dolls!

QUEEN'S BALL COOKIES
(AS SEEN ON PAGE 36)

4 cups coconut
4 cups pecans or hazelnuts
1 can Eagle Brand milk
1½ sticks butter or margarine
1 box powdered sugar
Chocolate for dipping

❀ Melt the butter. When it is melted, add the milk and sugar and mix well. Mince the pecans or hazelnuts until fine. Add the nuts and coconut to the butter and sugar mixture.

Refrigerate for 2 hours or overnight. When the dough has solidified, make into balls and refrigerate again.

Melt the chocolate. Dip balls in dipping chocolate until coated. Place on a wax-lined cookie sheet and cool until chocolate sets.

ENCHANTED BARK CANDY

1 bag white chocolate
    melting wafers
2 cups broken pretzel sticks
1 cup unsalted peanuts
1 cup small colored
    marshmallows

❀ Microwave the chocolate wafers in a microwave-safe large bowl at medium high for approximately 2 minutes, stirring one time. When the chocolate is melted, add the remaining ingredients and stir until everything is coated with the chocolate.

Spread on a large cookie sheet lined with wax paper. Refrigerate for 20 minutes until hard. Break into pieces. Stores well in an airtight container.

CHOCOLATE CHERRY FAIRY DROPS

3 tablespoons melted butter
1oz unsweetened chocolate
2 tablespoons half and half or canned milk
2 cup confectioner's sugar
10oz jar of cherries with stems
1lb white chocolate
1 cup colored chocolate

❀ To make the dough, in a large bowl mix together the butter, unsweetened chocolate, and half and half. When combined, add the confectioner's sugar.

Wrap the dough around the cherries, leaving steps at top. Put in refrigerator until they are cold.

Melt white chocolate, dip cherries until covered. Let cool. Melt contrasting color and drizzle over cherries. Let cool.

Glossary and Techniques

Abbreviations

APPROX	approximately
BEG	begin(ning)
CC	contrasting color
CH	chain
CM	centimeter(s)
CN	cable needle
CONT	continu(e)(ing)
DEC	decreas(e)(ing)
DPN	double-pointed needle(s)
FOLL	follow(s)(ing)
G	gram(s)
INC	increase(e)(ing)
K	knit
LH	left-hand
LP(S)	loop(s)
M	meter(s)
MM	millimeter(s)
MC	main color
M1	make one
M1 P-ST	make 1 purl stitch
OZ	ounce(s)
P	purl
PAT(S)	pattern(s)
PM	place marker
PSSO	pass slip stitch(es) over
REM	remain(s)(ing)
REP	repeat
RH	right-hand
RS	right side(s)
RND(S)	round(s)
SKP	slip 1, knit 1, pass slip stitch over—one stitch has been decreased
SK2P	slip 1, knit 2 together, pass slip stitch over the knit 2 together—two stitches have been decreased
S2KP	slip 2 stitches together, knit 1, pass 2 slip stitches over knit 1
SL	slip
SL ST	slip stitch
SSK	slip, slip, knit
SSSK	slip, slip, slip, knit
ST(S)	stitch(es)
ST ST	stockinette stitch
TBL	through back loop(s)
TOG	together
WS	wrong side(s)
W&T	wrap & turn

Standard Yarn Weight System

Categories of yarn, gauge ranges, and recommended needle and hook sizes

Yarn Weight Symbol & Category Names	**0** Lace	**1** Super Fine	**2** Fine	**3** Light	**4** Medium	**5** Bulky	**6** Super Bulky
Type of Yarns in Category	Fingering 10 count crochet thread	Sock, Fingering, Baby	Sport, Baby	DK, Light Worsted	Worsted, Afghan, Aran	Chunky, Craft, Rug	Bulky, Roving
Knit Gauge Range* in Stockinette Stitch to 4 inches	33–40** sts	27–32 sts	23–26 sts	21–24 sts	16–20 sts	12–15 sts	6–11 sts
Recommended Needle in Metric Size Range	1.5–2.25 mm	2.25–3.25 mm	3.25–3.75 mm	3.75–4.5 mm	4.5–5.5 mm	5.5–8 mm	8 mm and larger
Recommended Needle U.S. Size Range	000 to 1	1 to 3	3 to 5	5 to 7	7 to 9	9 to 11	11 and larger
Crochet Gauge* Ranges in Single Crochet to 4 inch	32-42 double crochets**	21–32 sts	16–20 sts	12–17 sts	11–14 sts	8–11 sts	5–9 sts
Recommended Hook in Metric Size Range	Steel*** 1.6–1.4mm Regular hook 2.25 mm	2.25–3.5 mm	3.5–4.5 mm	4.5–5.5 mm	5.5–6.5 mm	6.5–9 mm	9 mm and larger
Recommended Hook U.S. Size Range	Steel*** 6, 7, 8 Regular hook B–1	B–1 to E–4	E–4 to 7	7 to I–9	I–9 to K–10½	K–10½ to M–13	M–13 and larger

* GUIDELINES ONLY: The above reflect the most commonly used gauges and needle or hook sizes for specific yarn categories.

** Lace weight yarns are usually knitted or crocheted on larger needles and hooks to create lacy, openwork patterns. Accordingly, a gauge range is difficult to determine. Always follow the gauge stated in your pattern.

*** Steel crochet hooks are sized differently from regular hooks--the higher the number, the smaller the hook, which is the reverse of regular hook sizing.

This Standards & Guidelines booklet and downloadable symbol artwork are available at: **YarnStandards.com**

WYIB	with yarn in back
WYIF	with yarn in front
YD	yard(s)
YO	yarn over needle
*	repeat directions following * as many times as indicated
[ ]	repeat directions inside brackets as many times as indicated

Glossary

BIND OFF Used to finish an edge or segment. Lift the first stitch over the second, the second over the third, etc. (U.K.: cast off)

BIND OFF IN RIBBING Work in ribbing as you bind off. (Knit the knit stitches, purl the purl stitches.) (U.K.: cast off in ribbing)

3-NEEDLE BIND-OFF With the right side of the two pieces facing and the needles parallel, insert a third needle into the first stitch on each needle and knit them together. Knit the next two stitches the same way. Slip the first stitch on the third needle over the second stitch and off the needle. Repeat for three-needle bind-off.

CAST ON Placing a foundation row of stitches upon the needle in order to begin knitting.

DECREASE Reduce the stitches in a row (that is, knit 2 together).

INCREASE Add stitches in a row (that is, knit in front and back of stitch).

KNITWISE Insert the needle into the stitch as if you were going to knit it.

MAKE ONE With the needle tip, lift the strand between the last stitch knit and the next stitch on the left-hand needle and knit into back of it. One knit stitch has been added.

MAKE ONE P-ST With the needle tip, lift the strand between the last stitch worked and the next stitch on the left-hand needle and purl it. One purl stitch has been added.

PICK UP AND KNIT (PURL) Knit (or purl) into the loops along an edge.

PLACE MARKERS Place or attach a loop of contrast yarn or purchased stitch marker as indicated.

PURLWISE Insert the needle into the stitch as if you were going to purl it.

SELVAGE STITCH Edge stitch that helps make seaming easier.

SLIP, SLIP, KNIT Slip next two stitches knitwise, one at a time, to right-hand needle. Insert tip of left-hand needle into fronts of these stitches, from left to right. Knit them together. One stitch has been decreased.

SLIP, SLIP, SLIP, KNIT Slip next three stitches knitwise, one at a time, to right-hand needle. Insert tip of left-hand needle into fronts of these stitches, from left to right. Knit them together. Two stitches have been decreased.

SLIP STITCH Pass an unworked stitch from the left-hand to the right-hand needle purlwise.

WORK EVEN Continue in pattern without increasing or decreasing. (U.K.: work straight)

YARN OVER Making a new stitch by wrapping the yarn over the right-hand needle. (U.K.: yfwd, yon, yrn)

• •

Duplicate Stitch covers a knit stitch. Bring the needle up below the stitch to be worked. Insert the needle under both loops one row above and pull it through. Insert it back into the stitch below and through the center of the next stitch in one motion, as shown.

Duplicate stitch
used for
Skullduggery
page 51

How to Make a Pompom

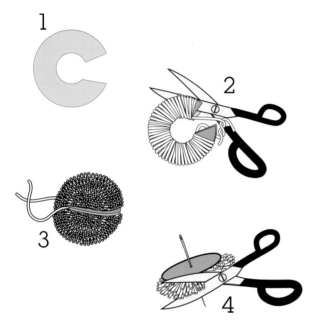

1

2

3

4

1 With two circular pieces of cardboard the width of the desired pompom, cut a center hole. Then cut a pie-shaped wedge out of the circle. (Use the picture as a guide.)

2 Hold the two circles together and wrap the yarn tightly around the cardboard. Then carefully cut around the cardboard.

3 Tie a piece of yarn tightly between the two circles. Remove the cardboard and trim the pompom.

4 Sandwich pompom between two round pieces of cardboard held together with a long needle. Cut around the circumference for a perfect pompom.

Pompom used in
Vintage Bunny
page 74

Embroidery Stitches

Embroidery used in
Fetching in Flowers
page 110

CHAIN STITCH

LAZY DAISY
STITCH

FRENCH KNOT

STEM STITCH

STRAIGHT STITCH

Kitchener Stitch

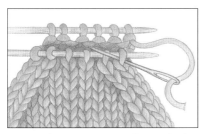

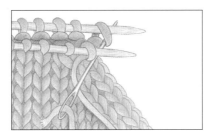

1 Insert tapestry needle purlwise (as shown) through first stitch on front needle. Pull yarn through, leaving that stitch on knitting needle.

2 Insert tapestry needle knitwise (as shown) through first stitch on back needle. Pull yarn through, leaving stitch on knitting needle.

Kitchener stitch used in Ruffles and Roses page 14

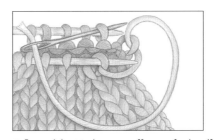

3 Insert tapestry needle knitwise through first stitch on front needle, slip stitch off needle and insert tapestry needle purlwise (as shown) through next stitch on front needle. Pull yarn through, leaving this stitch on needle.

4 Insert tapestry needle purlwise through first stitch on back needle. Slip stitch off needle and insert tapestry needle knitwise (as shown) through next stitch on back needle. Pull yarn through, leaving this stitch on needle. Repeat steps 3 and 4 until all stitches on both front and back needles have been grafted. Fasten off and weave in end.

Three-Needle Bind-Off
This bind-off is used to join two edges that have the same number of stitches, such as shoulder edges which have been placed on holders.

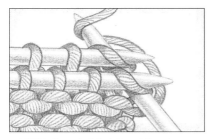

1 With the right side of the two pieces facing each other, and the needles parallel, insert a third needle knitwise into the first stitch of each needle. Wrap the yarn around the needle as if to knit.

2 Knit these two stitches together and slip them off the needles. *Knit the next two stitches together in the same way as shown.

3 Slip the first stitch on the third needle over the second stitch and off the needle. Repeat from the * in step 2 across the row until all the stitches are bound off.

I-cord

Cast on about three to five stitches. *Knit one row. Without turning the work, slip the stitches back to the beginning of the row. Pull the yarn tightly from the end of the row. Repeat from the * as desired. Bind off.

I-cord used on hat of
A Rose Is a Rose
page 30

Beading

1 When threading beads onto yarn, the needle must be large enough to accommodate the yarn, but small enough to go through the beads. You can use an auxilliary thread, as shown here. Loop the thread through a folded piece of yarn and pull both ends through.

2 To add beads in stockinette stitch on right-side rows, beads are placed without the purl stitches on either side. The bead will lie directly in front of the stitch. Work the stitch firmly so that the bead won't fall to the back of the work.

3 From the right side: Work to the stitch to be beaded, then slip the bead up in back of the work. Insert needle as if to knit; wrap yarn around it. Push bead to front through the stitch on the left needle; complete the stitch.

Beading
used in
Mirror, Mirror
page 44

Yarn Resources

AUNT LYDIA'S
a Coats & Clark Brand

CASCADE YARNS
1224 Andover Park East
Tukwila, WA 98188
www.cascadeyarns.com

COATS & CLARK
PO Box 12229
Greenville, SC 29612
tel: (800) 648-1479
www.coatsandclark.com

CRYSTAL PALACE YARNS
Straw into Gold, Inc.
160 23rd Street
Richmond, CA 94804
www.straw.com

DEBBIE BLISS
Distributed by Knitting Fever
www.debbieblissonline.com

DMC
10 Basin Drive
Suite 130
Kearny, NJ 07032
Tel: (973) 589-0606
www.dmc-usa.com

FILATURA DI CROSA
Distributed by Tahki▪Stacy
Charles, Inc.

KNITTING FEVER (KFI)
PO Box 336
315 Bayview Avenue
Amityville, NY 11701
www.knittingfever.com

KOIGU WOOL DESIGNS
PO Box 158
Chatsworth, Ontario N0H1G0
Canada
Tel: (888) 765-WOOL (765-9665)
www.koigu.com

LION BRAND YARN CO.
34 West 15th Street
New York, NY 10011
www.lionbrand.com

LUCCI YARNS
202-91 Rocky Hill Road
Bayside, NY 11361
Tel: (718) 281-0119
lucciyarn.com

PRISM YARNS
www.prismyarn.com

RED HEART LTD.
a Coats & Clark Brand
www.redheart.com

ROZETTI YARNS
a Universal Yarn Inc. Brand
Sassy Skein
Tel: (239) 995-9441
www.sassyskein.com

SCHACHENMAYR SMC
us.knitsmc.com/smc

TAHKI▪STACY CHARLES, INC.
70-60 83rd Street, Building #12
Glendale, NY 11385
www.tahkistacycharles.com

TILLI TOMAS
Tel: (617) 524-3330
www.tillitomas.com

UNIVERSAL YARN INC.
284 Ann Street
Concord, NC 28025
Tel: (877) Uni-Yarn (864-9276)
www.universalyarn.com

YARN RESOURCES IN
THE UK AND EUROPE

GRIGNASCO KNITS
Via Dante Alighieri n. 2
28075 Grignasco, Novara
Italy
Tel: +39 0163 4101
www.grignascoknits.it

SIRDAR SPINNING LTD
Flanshaw Lane
Wakefield, West Yorkshire
WF2 9ND
United Kingdom
Tel: +44(0) 1924 371501
www.sirdar.co.uk

Handcrafted wooden
dollhouse, page 75
by BENSON MTN CABINETS
bensonmountaincabinets.com

Project Index

Acknowledgments

It takes a village—or in this case a dollhouse—full of very talented and hard-working publishing pros at Sixth&Spring to make a book!

I want to thank for their benevolence the godfathers, Art Joinnides and Jay Stein, who made me an offer that I could refuse, but didn't!

Many thanks to Trisha Malcolm and Carla Scott for their ongoing support, encouragement, and talent.

My fantastic editor, Joy Aquilino (a real doll).

Diane Lamphron, art director extraordinaire, for her artistic flair and her patience in putting up with me.

Jack Deutsch (the guy among the dolls) and his team, who got the dolls to stand and pose for his always lovely photos. I swear, when he said "say cheese" . . . they smiled!

Johanna Levy, the stylist whose contributions to clothing, hair, and other elements helped bring the dolls to life.

Lisa Silverman, our hard-working developmental editor, whose descriptive prose captured the essence of the garments.

Christina Behnke, our yarn editor, who beautifully matched the right yarn to the right doll.

Sandi Prosser, Nancy Henderson, and Lori Steinberg, our eagle-eyed technical editors and proofreaders.

Amy Polcyn, our intelligent and capable pattern writer.

David Joinnides, a boy doll!

Mary Taylor, for her support and great idea for the back cover.

Thanks to my intrepid knitters, with their little needles and big hearts, who made my deadlines and kept me in stitches: Nancy Henderson, Jo Brandon, and Deanna Van Assche.

Thanks to the generous folks at JHB International, who supplied all the lovely buttons.

Thanks also to Alexander Doll Company, a division of KLL Dolls, LLC, for contributing their beautiful dolls to our photography.

And thank you to all the little people . . . of course, I mean the dolls! ✿

OTHER KNITTING
AND CROCHET
BOOKS BY
NICKY EPSTEIN

Cover Up with
Nicky Epstein

Crocheting on the Edge

Knitting a Kiss in
Every Stitch

Knitting Beyond
the Edge

Knitting on the Edge

Knitting Over the Edge

Knitting Never
Felt Better

Nicky Epstein
Crochet for Dolls

Nicky Epstein
Crocheted Flowers

Nicky Epstein
Knitted Flowers

Nicky Epstein Knitting
in Tuscany

Nicky Epstein Knitting
on Top of the World

Nicky Epstein
The Essential Edgings
Collection

Nicky Epstein's
Signature Scarves

Nicky
Epstein
Books

an imprint of

sixth&spring
books

sixthandspringbooks.com

Now we're all dressed up and ready to go!